ISBN 978-1-332-75763-3
PIBN 10432933

1 MONTH OF
FREE
READING

at

www.ForgottenBooks.com

By purchasing this book you are eligible for one month membership to ForgottenBooks.com, giving you unlimited access to our entire collection of over 700,000 titles via our web site and mobile apps.

To claim your free month visit:
www.forgottenbooks.com/free432933

OLD ENGLISH PLAYS No. 2

Heywood's
A Woman Killed with Kindness

Works by F. J. Cox

A STRANGER WITHIN THE GATES, A Story
of Severn Side. Crown 8vo. Cloth, 6s.

SONGS OF THE CAR, with "De Omnibus" Rhymes.
Illustrated by Howard Somerville. Crown 8vo.
Cloth, 3s. 6d. net.

London: Francis Griffiths

A Woman Killed with Kindness

by Thomas Heywood

Edited, with Introduction and Notes, by F. J. Cox.

Published by FRANCIS GRIFFITHS at the Sign of the Gryphon, 34 Maiden Lane, near the Strand, in the City of Westminster MDCCCCVII

OLD ENGLISH PLAYS

Paper, **6d.** net.　　Cloth, **1s.** net.

1. **The Tragical History of Doctor Faustus.** By CHRISTOPHER MARLOWE.
2. **A Woman Killed with Kindness.** By THOMAS HEYWOOD.
3. **Every Man in his Humour.** By BEN JONSON.
4. **The Maid's Tragedy.** By FRANCIS BEAUMONT and JOHN FLETCHER.

London: FRANCIS GRIFFITHS

THE PLAY .
AND . . . .
ITS AUTHOR.

PERHAPS, of all the dramatists of the Elizabethan and Jacobean epochs, Thomas Heywood is one of the least known to the mass of readers. To many, doubtless, he is scarcely a name even, and the most diligent student of our literary byways would probably be hard put to it to identify him as the author of "Fortune by Land and Sea," or that quaintly-named play, "If you know not Me, you know Nobody." But if his works have remained "caviare to the general," they have been fondly prized and read with delight by men of letters from Charles Lamb downwards. Just as Spencer has been called "the poet's poet," so Thomas· Heywood may, in a more limited sense, be described as "the litterateur's playwright." But there is no valid reason why his appeal should be thus circumscribed. His plays, so far from being academic, stilted, or abstruse, smelling of the lamp rather than the sweet air of the country-side, are full of sheer humanity, studied at first hand and portrayed with skilful force through the medium of dramatic art.

depths of passion; Christianism, and true hearty Anglicism of feelings, shaping that Christianism, shine throughout his beautiful writings in a manner more conspicuous than in those of Shakespeare; but only more conspicuous, inasmuch as in Heywood these qualities are primary, in the other subordinate to poetry." The tribute paid by Charles Lamb to the genius of his " prose Shakespeare " has been followed by the unstinted eulogies of other literary critics. Hazlitt says that " his imagination is a gentle lambent flame that purifies without consuming." His dialogue he describes as " beautiful prose put into heroic measure." Robert Louis Stevenson swells the chorus of praise by declaring that, if Heywood was not an immortal, he was at least an " immortalette." Mr. J. Addington Symonds remarks that he " is essentially an author whom we love the better the more we read of him. It is impossible to rise from the perusal of his plays without being refreshed and invigorated."

Of the life of Heywood little is known. He shares the obscurity common to most of the great Elizabethans. From the meagre records of his career that are available, we gather that he was born in Lincolnshire probably some ten or twelve years later than Shakespeare and Marlowe. After a residence at Cambridge, he came to London, there to enter upon his life-work as a writer and actor of plays. He was first of all attached to the Lord Admiral's Company of Players, then to the Earl of Worcester's, and finally, on the accession of James I., to the

Queen's.   The famous Henslowe was his col-
league, and for a time, his chief.   The following
extract from that actor's diary is interesting as
showing, for one thing, that the modern maker
of plays has no cause to envy the emoluments
of his Elizabethan predecessor :

> " Paid, at the Appointment of the Company
> the 6th of March, 1602, unto Thomas Hey-
> wood, in full payment for his Play called ' A
> Woman Kill'd with Kindness.' . . . . . £3. "

Such fragmentary records, and the internal evidence furnished by the plays themselves, give
us all we know of the life of Thomas Heywood.
Even the date of his death is unknown.

One of the most striking characteristics of
Heywood's genius is its amazing fruitfulness.
Most of his contemporaries were voluminous
producers, but he excels them all.   Those were
the days when men were not afraid to speak out,
for no imp of self-criticism sat at their elbows.
Facility they had in brimming measure, but it
was not of necessity fatal, for the right word
seemed to leap to their lips spontaneously, and
their glorious lyrical cadences flowed from them
with an impromptu rush.   They spurned the
services of the file, and would have scorned the
assiduous craftsman who spent a whole night
in polishing a single line.   Heywood went at his
work impetuously and without cessation.   It was
his rule never to let a day pass without writing
something.   He observed this rule rigidly, and

neither the mood nor the place he was in seemed to have any effect upon the flow of his thoughts and the expression of them. Some of his plays were written on odd scraps of paper, the backs of tavern bills being often pressed into service. This carelessness resulted in the loss of many of the plays, and the capture of others by the literary pirates of the day, whose depredations went unrestrained and unpunished by any copyright law. Of the 220 plays in which Heywood declares he had " an entire hand or, at the least, a main finger," only 24 have been preserved. Nor did dramatic composition exhaust all his time or consume all his energies; he was not only a playwright, but a literary man, quite in the modern sense of the term, whose superabundant activities were employed in the writing of histories, dictionaries of poets, or anything else that happened to come his way.

By universal consent " A Woman Killed with Kindness " has been adjudged the best of Thomas Heywood's plays. It shows, for one thing, what an enormous advance had been made in the Anglicising of the drama since Marlowe's time. This tendency did not make for insular narrowness but for faithfulness in portraying things actually observed. Heywood painted the men and women around him as he saw them. His dramas are a mirror of the times they were written in. They are more peculiarly English than those of Shakespeare, who so often gave his comedies a foreign setting, and occupied himself in his historical pageants with the fortunes

cacies of plot, being a plain, unvarnished story of a woman's frailty and a man's duplicity. It is, in fine, a tragedy of two men and one woman. Though more than three hundred years have elapsed since the play was written, it has retained all its freshness and all its power to touch the emotions. There are at least two scenes in the drama which are full of unescapable pathos—that wherein Mistress Frankford is confronted by her two children after her husband's discovery of her guilt, and the death scene at the close. The one blemish of the play, its one psychological fault, is the ease with which the woman falls. It is hardly conceivable that Anne Frankford, married to so excellent a husband, and with the heyday of the honeymoon hardly over, would have proved such an easy prey to the machinations of Wendoll. Neither are we quite persuaded that a woman who sinned so lightly, and resisted so half-heartedly the proposals of her seducer, would have been so absolutely overwhelmed by remorse and despair when her secret was discovered. The victim of selfish indulgence as she seems to be, she would, we think, have clung tenaciously to life at all costs. But the treatment of Anne Frankford was Heywood's way with erring woman. Mistress Wincott, the heroine of "The English Traveller," sacrifices her chastity from a motive equally inadequate, and when found out, repents and dies in the same mechanical manner. But it must not be supposed that all Heywood's women are weak-willed, and wantons at heart. Bess Bridges, in "The Fair

Maid of the West," is a striking instance to the contrary; she is a spirited girl with a man's courage and a woman's devotion to her absent lover.

The story of " A Woman Killed with Kindness " hardly requires further summarisation. Its narrative is so plain that all who run may read.   It contains no entanglements to be unravelled, no ambiguities to be elucidated, and few archaic words to be explained.   In accordance with Heywood's general method, the play has a secondary plot; the misfortunes of Sir Charles Mountford and his sister Susan blend well with the tragic history of the Frankfords, and impart a touch of fulness and completion to the drama. The direct and unrhetorical diction of the play shows what splendid dignity, simplicity, and reserve had been attained by Marlowe's successors in the use of the instrument which that mighty master of dramatic harmonies had devised.   Arresting passages abound in the play, and will be found readily enough by the discerning reader.   Grace and melody meet together in Mistress Frankford's reference to her husband immediately after the bridal :

" His sweet content is like a flattering glass,
    To make my face seem fairer to mine eye;"

and her brother's description of herself, as a wife,

" Pliant and duteous in your husband's love."

Wendoll's impassioned declaration of his illicit love issues with torrential force from his lips:

             " O speak no more!
For more than this I know, and have recorded
Within the red-leaved table of my heart.
Fair, and of all beloved, I was not fearful
Bluntly to give my life into your hand,
And at one hazard all my earthly means.
Go, tell your husband; he will turn me off,
And I am then undone. I care not, I;
'Twas for your sake. Perchance in rage he'll
   kill me :
I care not, 'twas for you. Say I incur
The general name of villain through the world,
Of traitor to my friend; I care not, I.
Beggary, shame, death, scandal, and reproach,
For you I'll hazard all."

In the following moving lines Frankford expresses the first agony of his soul after the discovery of his wife's adultery:

     " O God! O God! that it were possible
To undo things done; to call back yesterday!
That time could turn up his swift sandy
   glass,
To untell the days, and to redeem these
   hours !
Or that the sun
Could, rising from the west, draw his coach
   backward,

Take from the account of time so many
    minutes,
Till he had all these seasons called again,
Those minutes, and those actions done in
    them,
Even from her first offence; that I might
    take her
As spotless as an angel in my arms!
But, oh! I talk of things impossible,
And cast beyond the moon. God give me
    patience!
For I will in and wake them."

The great forgiveness of which the soul of the
injured Frankford is capable finds vent in a
passage of noble eloquence:

" My wife, the mother to my pretty babes!
Both those lost names I do restore thee back,
And with this kiss I wed thee once again:
Though thou art wounded in thy honoured
    name,
And with that grief upon thy death-bed liest,
Honest in heart, upon my soul, thou diest."

It is to be hoped that the reader will not allow
his studies of Heywood's works to stop short
at the present drama; he will find in many of
the remaining twenty-three plays much moving
story and eloquent verse. For Heywood is one
of the dramatists who belie the crabbed dictum
of Walter Savage Landor that Shakespeare's
contemporaries were mushrooms that sprang up

about the roots of the oak of Arden. They are
rather, in Mr. Swinburne's splendid phrase,
" gulfs or estuaries of the sea which is Shakespeare."

In the present reprint the text contained in
Heywood's collected plays, published by Pearson
in 1874, has been followed. Previous to this,
in 1850, the Shakespearian Society published an
edition, under the editorship of Payne Collier.
The Pearson reprint should be consulted by those
who wish to obtain a complete knowledge of the
dramatist, but the five selected plays in the
" Mermaid " series will form a useful introduction to the larger study of the poet.

F. J. COX.

THE PROLOGUE

I COME but like a Harbinger, being sent
  To tell you what these preparations mean:
Look for no glorious state, our Muse is bent
  Upon a barren subject: a bare scene.
We could afford this twig a Timber tree,
  Whose strength might boldly on your favours
    build;
Our Russet, Tissue; Drone, a Honey-Bee;
  Our barren plot, a large and spacious field;
Our coarse fare, banquets; our thin Water,
  Wine;
  Our Brook, a Sea; our Bat's eyes, Eagle's
    sight;
Our Poet's dull and earthy Muse, Divine;
  Our Ravens, Doves; our Crow's black feathers,
    white.
But gentle thoughts when they may give the foil,
Save them that yield, and spare where they may
  spoil.

DRAMATIS PERSONÆ

Sir FRANCIS ACTON, Brother of ANNE FRANKFORD.
Sir CHARLES MOUNTFORD.
Master JOHN FRANKFORD.
Master WENDOLL, Friend to FRANKFORD.
Master MALBY, Friend to Sir FRANCIS.
Master CRANWELL.
SHAFTON, a False Friend to Sir CHARLES.
OLD MOUNTFORD, Uncle to Sir CHARLES.
TIDY, Cousin to Sir CHARLES.
SANDY.
RODER.
NICHOLAS,
JENKIN,
ROGER BRICKBAT, } Servants to FRANKFORD.
JACK SLIME,
SPIGOT, a Butler,
Sheriff.
A Serjeant, a Keeper, Officers, Falconers, Hunts-
men, a Coachman, Carters, Servants, Musicians.
ANNE FRANKFORD.
SUSAN, Sister of Sir CHARLES.
CICELY, Maid to Mistress FRANKFORD.
Women Servants.

A Woman Killed with Kindness

SCENE—The North of England.

Enter Master John Frankford, Mistress Anne Frankford, Sir Francis Acton, Sir Charles Mountford, Master Malby, Master Wendoll, *and* Master Cranwell.

Sir Fran. Some music there. None lead the the bride a dance?

Sir Char. Yes, would she dance *The Shaking of the Sheets?*[1]

But that's the dance her husband means to lead her?

Wen. That's not the dance that every man must dance,

According to the Ballad.

I should have said—the hand that but this day

Was given you in the church I'll borrow : Sound !

This marriage music hoists me from the ground.

Frank. Ay, you may caper, you are light and free :

Marriage hath yoked my heels ; pray then pardon me.

[1] The name of a popular tune, to which many ballads of the time were written.

Sir Fran. I'll have you dance too, brother.
Sir Char. Master Frankford,
You are a happy man, sir, and much joy
Succeed your marriage mirth. You have a wife
So qualified, and with such ornaments
Both of the mind and body. First, her birth
Is noble, and her education such
As might become the daughter of a Prince:
Her own tongue speaks all tongues, and her own
    hand
Can teach all strings to speak in their best grace
From the shrillest treble to the hoarsest base.
To end her many praises in one word,
She's beauty and perfection's eldest daughter,
Only found by yours, though many a heart hath
    sought her.
    Frank. But that I know your virtues and
    chaste thoughts,
I should be jealous of your praise, Sir Charles.
    Cran. He speaks no more than you approve.
    Mal. Nor flatters he that gives to her her due.
    Anne. I would your praise could find a fitter
    theme
Than my imperfect beauties to speak on;
Such as they be, if they my husband please,
They suffice me now I am marri èd:
His sweet content is like a flattering glass,
To make my face seem fairer to mine eye;
But the least wrinkle from his stormy brow
Will blast the roses in my cheeks that grow.
    Sir Fran. A perfect wife already, meek and
    patient;
How strangely the word "husband" fits your
    mouth,
Not married three hours since! Sister, 'tis good;
You, that begin betimes thus, must needs prove
Pliant and duteous in your husband's love.—

Gramercies, brother, wrought her to it already;
Sweet husband, and a curtsey, the first day!
Mark this, mark this, you that are bachelors,
And never took the grace of honest man;
Mark this, against you marry, this one phrase:
" In a good time that man both wins and woos,
That takes his wife down in her wedding shoes."

 Frank. Your sister takes not after you, Sir
  Francis;
All his wild blood your father spent on you:
He got her in his age, when he grew civil;
All his mad tricks were to his land entailed,
And you are heir to all; your sister, she
Hath to her dower her mother's modesty.

 Sir Char. Lord, sir, in what a happy state live
  you;
This morning, which to many seems a burden
Too heavy to bear, is unto you a pleasure.
This lady is no clog, as many are:
She doth become you like a well-made suit,
In which the tailor hath used all his art:
Not like a thick coat of unseasoned frieze,
Forced on your back in summer. She's no chain
To tie your neck, and curb you to the yoke;
But she's a chain of gold to adorn your neck.
You both adorn each other, and your hands,
Methinks, are matches: there's equality
In this fair combination; you are both
Scholars, both young, both being descended
 nobly.
There's music in this sympathy; it carries
Consort, and expectation of much joy, .
Which God bestow on you, from this first day
Until your dissolution—that's for aye.

 Sir Fran. We keep you here too long, good
  brother Frankford.
Into the hall; away, go cheer your guests!

What! bride and bridegroom both withdrawn
    at once?
If you be missed, the guests will doubt their
    welcome,
And charge you with unkindness.
    Frank. To prevent it,
I'll leave you here, to see the dance within.
    Anne. And so will I.
[*Exeunt* FRANKFORD *and* Mistress FRANKFORD.
    Sir Fran. To part you it were sin.
Now gallants, while the town-musicians
Finger their frets² within; and the mad lads
And country-lasses, every mother's child,
With nosegays and bridelaces in their hats,
Dance all their country measures, rounds, and
    jigs,
What shall we do? Hark, they are all on the
    hoigh;³
They toil like mill-horses, and turn as round,—
Marry, not on the toe. Ay, and they caper,
Not without cutting: you shall see to-morrow
The hall-floor pecked and dinted like a mill-stone,
Made with their high shoes: though their skill
    be small,
Yet they tread heavy where their hob-nails fall.
    Sir Char. Well, leave them to their sports.
    Sir Francis Acton,
I'll make a match with you: meet to-morrow
At Chevy-chase, I'll fly my hawk with yours.
    Sir Fran. For what? For what?
    Sir Char. Why, for a hundred pound.
    Sir Fran. Pawn me some gold of that.
    Sir Char. Here are ten angels;⁴

₂The strings of a lute, guitar, etc.

₃On the romp.

₄An angel: a gold coin varying in value from 6/8 to 1/0

I'll make them good a hundred pound to-morrow
Upon my hawk's wing.

Sir Fran. 'Tis a match, 'tis done.
Another hundred pound upon your dogs;
Dare ye, Sir Charles?

Sir Char. I dare: were I sure to lose,
I durst do more than that: here's my hand,
The first course for a hundred pound.

Sir Fran. A match.

Wen. Ten angels on Sir Francis Acton's hawk;
As much upon his dogs.

  Cran. I am for Sir Charles Mountford; I have
    seen
His hawk and dog both tried. What, clap you
    hands?
Or is't no bargain?

  Wen. Yes, and stake them down:
Were they five hundred, they were all my own.

  Sir Fran. Be stirring early with the lark to-
    morrow;
I'll rise into my saddle ere the sun
Rise from his bed.

  Sir Char. If there you miss me, say
I am no gentleman. I'll hold my day.

  Sir Fran. It holds on all sides. Come, to-night
    let's dance,
Early to-morrow let's prepare to ride;
We had need be three hours up before the bride.
                        [Exeunt.

Enter NICHOLAS *and* JENKIN, JACK SLIME, *and*
    ROGER BRICKBAT, *with* Country Wenches,
    and two or three Musicians.

Jenk. Come, Nick, take you Joan Miniver to
trace withal; Jack Slime, traverse you with

Cicely Milk-pail: I will take Jane Trubkin, and
Roger Brickbat shall have Isbel Motley; and now
that they are busy in the parlour, come, strike
up; we'll have a crash[5] here in the yard.

Nic. My humour is not compendious; dancing
I possess not, though I can foot it; yet, since
I am fallen into the hands of Cicely Milk-pail,
I consent.

Jack. Truly Nick, though we were never
brought up like serving courtiers, yet we have
been brought up with serving creatures, ay, and
God's creatures too; for we have been brought
up to serve sheep, oxen, horses, hogs, and such
like: and, though we be but country fellows, it
may be in the way of dancing we can do the
horse-trick as well as serving-men.

Roger. Ay, and the cross-point too.

Jenk. O Slime, O Brickbat, do not you know
that comparisons are odious? now we are odious
ourselves too, therefore there are no comparisons
to be made betwixt us.

Nic. I am sudden, and not superfluous:
I am quarrelsome, and not seditious:
I am peaceable, and not contentious:
I am brief, and not compendious.

Jack. Foot it quickly; if the music overcome
not my melancholy, I shall quarrel; and if they
do not suddenly strike up, I shall presently strike
them down.

Jenk. No quarrelling, for God's sake! Truly,
if you do, I shall set a knave between ye.

Jack. I come to dance, not to quarrel. Come,
what shall it be? *Rogero?*

Jenk. Rogero, no; we will dance *The Begin-
ning of the World.*

---

5 Crash: a feast, an entertainment.

Cicely. I love no dance so well as *John come kiss me now.*

Nic. I that have ere now deserved a cushion, call for the *Cushion-dance.*

Roger. For my part, I like nothing so well as *Tom Tyler.*

Jenk. No; we'll have *The Hunting of the Fox.*

Jack. The Hay, The Hay; there's nothing like *The Hay.*

Nic. I have said, I do say, and I will say again—

Jenk. Every man agree to have it as Nick says.

All. Content.

Nic. It hath been, it now is, and it shall be—

Cicely. What, Master Nicholas, what?

Nic. Put on your smock a' Monday.

Jenk. So the dance will come cleanly off. Come, for God's sake agree of something: if you like not that, put it to the musicians; or let me speak for all, and we'll have *Sellenger's round.*

All. That, that, that.

Nic. No, I am resolved, thus it shall be: First take hands, then take ye to your heels.

Jenk. Why, would ye have us run away?

Nic. No; but I would have you shake your heels.

Music, strike up!

> [*They dance.* Nicholas *whilst dancing speaks stately and scurvily, the rest after the country fashion.*

Jenk. Hey! lively, my lasses! here's a turn for thee! [*Exeunt.*

Wind horns. Enter Sir Charles, Sir Francis, Malby, Cranwell, Wendoll, Falconer, *and* Huntsmen.

Sir Char. So; well cast off : aloft, aloft ! well
  flown !
Oh, now she takes her at the sowse, and strikes
  her
Down to the earth, like a swift thunder-clap.
  Wen. She hath struck ten angels out of my
  way.
Sir Fran. A hundred pound from me.
Sir Char. What, falconer !
Fal. At hand, sir.
Sir Char. Now she hath seized the fowl, and
  'gins to plume her,
Rebeck her not : rather stand still and check
  her.
So, seize her gets,⁶ her jesses,⁷ and her bells :
Away !
  Sir Fran. My hawk killed too.
  Sir Char. Ay, but 'twas at the querre,⁸
Not at the mount like mine.
  Sir Fran. Judgment, my masters.
  Cran. Yours missed her at the ferre.
  Wen. Ay, but our merlin first had plumed the
  fowl,
And twice renewed her from the river too;
Her bells, Sir Francis, had not both one weight,
Nor was one semi-tune above the other :
Methinks these Milan bells do sound too full,
And spoil the mounting of your hawk.
  Sir Char. 'Tis lost.
  Sir Fran. I grant it not. Mine likewise seized
  a fowl
Within her talons and you saw her paws
Full of the feathers : both her petty singles,

  ⁶ Gets : gains, booty.
  ⁷ Jesses were short leather straps round the hawk's legs
having little rings to which the falconer's leash was
fastened.
  ⁸ The meaning of this term in falconry is obscure.

And her long singles, gripped her more than
    other;
The terrials of her legs were stained with blood:
Not of the fowl only she did discomfit
Some of her feathers; but she brake away.
Come, come, your hawk is but a rifler.
    Sir Char. How!
    Sir Fran. Ay, and your dogs are trindle-tails
    and curs.
    Sir Char. You stir my blood.
You keep not one good hound in all your kennel,
Nor one good hawk upon your perch.
    Sir Fran. How, knight!
    Sir Char. So, knight: you will not swagger,
    sir?
    Sir Fran. Why, say I did?
    Sir Char. Why sir,
I say you would gain as much by swaggering,
As you have got by wagers on your dogs:
You will come short in all things.
    Sir Fran. Not in this:
Now I'll strike home.
    Sir Char. Thou shalt to thy long home,
Or I will want my will.
    Sir Fran. All they that love Sir Francis, follow
    me.
    Sir Char. All that affect Sir Charles draw on
my part.
    Cran. On this side heaves my hand.
    Wen. Here goes my heart.
    [*They divide themselves.* Sir CHARLES,
      CRANWELL, Falconer, *and* Huntsman,
      fight against Sir FRANCIS ACTON, WEN-
      DOLL, *his* Falconer, *and* Huntsman;
      and Sir CHARLES'S *side gets the better,
      beating them away, and killing both of*
      Sir FRANCIS' *men.*

Sir Char. My God! what have I done? what
    have I done?
My rage hath plunged into a sea of blood,
In which my soul lies drowned. Poor innocents,
For whom we are to answer! Well 'tis done,
And I remain the victor. A great conquest,
When I would give this right hand, nay, this
    head,
To breathe in them new life whom I have slain!
Forgive me, God! 'twas in the heat of blood,
And anger quite removes me from myself:
It was not I, but rage, did this vile murder;
Yet I, and not my rage, must answer it.
Sir Francis Acton he is fled the field;
With him all those that did partake his quarrel,
And I am left alone with sorrow dumb,
And in my height of conquest overcome.

Enter SUSAN.

Susan. O God! my brother wounded 'mong
    the dead!
Unhappy jest, that in such earnest ends;
The rumour of this fear stretched to my ears,
And I am come to know if you be wounded.
    Sir Char. Oh! sister, sister, wounded at the
    heart.
    Susan. My God forbid!
    Sir Char. In doing that thing which He forbad,
I am wounded, sister.
    Susan. I hope not at the heart.
    Sir Char. Yes, at the heart.
    Susan. O God! a surgeon there!
    Sir Char. Call me a surgeon, sister, for my
    soul;
The sin of murder it hath pierced my heart,
And made a wide wound there: but for these
    scratches,

They are nothing, nothing.
  Susan. Charles, what have you done?
Sir Francis hath great friends, and will pursue
    you
Unto the utmost danger of the law.
  Sir Char. My conscience is become mine,
    enemy,
And will pursue me more than Acton can.
  Susan. Oh, fly, sweet brother.
  Sir Char. Shall I fly from thee?
Why, Sue, art weary of my company?
  Susan. Fly from your foe.
  Sir Char. You, sister, are my friend;
And, flying you, I shall pursue my end.
  Susan. Your company is as my eye-ball dear;
Being far from you, no comfort can be near;
Yet fly to save your life; what would I care
To spend my future age in black despair,
So you were safe? and yet to live one week
Without my brother Charles, through every cheek
My streaming tears would downwards run so
    rank,
Till they could set on either side a bank,
And in the midst a channel; so my face
For two salt-water brooks shall still find place.
  Sir Char. Thou shalt not weep so much, for
    I will stay
In spite of danger's teeth; I'll live with thee,
Or I'll not live at all. I will not sell
My country and my father's patrimony,
Nor thy sweet sight, for a vain hope of life.

Enter Sheriff, *with* Officers.

  Sher. Sir Charles, I am made the unwilling
    instrument

Of your attach and apprehension:
I am sorry that the blood of innocent men
Should be of you exacted. It was told me
That you were guarded with a troop of friends,
And therefore I come thus armed.
  Sir Char. O Master Sheriff,
I came into the field with many friends,
But see, they all have left me: only one
Clings to my sad misfortune, my dear sister.
I know you for an honest gentleman;
I yield my weapons, and submit to you;
Convey me where you please.
  Sher. To prison then,
To answer for the lives of these dead men.
  Susan. O God! O God!
  Sir Char. Sweet sister, every strain
Of sorrow from your heart augments my pain;
Your grief abounds, and hits against my breast.
  Sher. Sir, will you go?
  Sir Char. Even where it likes you best.
                          [Exeunt.

Enter Master FRANKFORD *in* A STUDY.

  Frank. How happy am I amongst other men,
That in my mean estate embrace content.
I am a gentleman, and by my birth,
Companion with a king; a king's no more.
I am possessed of many fair revenues,
Sufficient to maintain a gentleman.
Touching my mind, I am studied in all arts;
The riches of my thoughts, and of my time,
Have been a good proficient; but the chief
Of all the sweet felicities on earth,

I have a fair, a chaste, and loving wife,
Perfection all, all truth, all ornament;
If man on earth may truly happy be,
Of these at once possessed, sure I am he.

Enter NICHOLAS.

Nic. Sir, there's a gentleman attends without
To speak with you.
Frank. On horseback?
Nic. Yes, on horseback.
Frank. Entreat him to alight, I will attend
him.
Know'st thou him, Nick?
Nic. Know him! yes, his name's Wendoll:
It seems he comes in haste; his horse is booted
Up to the flank in mire; himself all spotted
And stained with plashing. Sure he rid in fear
Or for a wager. Horse and man both sweat;
I ne'er saw two in such a smoking heat.
Frank. Entreat him in; about it instantly.
This Wendoll I have noted, and his carriage
Hath pleased me much: by observation
I have noted many good deserts in him:
He's affable, and seen' in many things,
Discourses well, a good companion;
And though of small means, yet a gentleman
Of a good house, though somewhat pressed by
want.
I have preferred him to a second place
In my opinion, and my best regard.

Enter WENDOLL, ANNE FRANKFORD, *and*
NICHOLAS.

Anne. O Master Frankford, Master Wendoll
here

9 Skilled.

Brings you the strangest news that e'er you
    heard.
   Frank. What news, sweet wife? What news,
        good Master Wendoll?
   Wen. You knew the match made 'twixt Sir
        Francis Acton
And Sir Charles Mountford?
   Frank. True, with their hounds and hawks.
   Wen. The matches were both played.
   Frank. Ha! and which won?
   Wen. Sir Francis, your wife's brother, had the
        worst,
And lost the wager.
   Frank. Why, the worse his chance :
Perhaps the fortune of some other day
Will change his luck.
   Anne. Oh, but you hear not all.
Sir Francis lost, and yet was loth to yield :
At length the two knights grew to difference,
From words to blows, and so to banding sides;
Where valorous Sir Charles slew in his spleen
Two of your brother's men : his falconer,
And his good huntsman, whom he loved so well :
More men were wounded, no more slain outright.
   Frank. Now, trust me, I am sorry for the
        knight;
But is my brother safe?
   Wen. All whole and sound,
His body not being blemished with one wound :
But poor Sir Charles is to the prison led,
To answer at the assize for them that's dead.
   Frank. I thank your pains, sir; had the news
        been better
Your will was to have brought it, Master Wen-
    doll.
Sir Charles will find hard friends; his case is
    heinous,

And will be most severely censured on:
I'm sorry for him.   Sir, a word with you;
I know you, sir, to be a gentleman
In all things; your possibilities but mean:
Please you to use my table and my purse,
They are yours.

    Wen. O Lord, sir, I shall never deserve it.

    Frank. O sir, disparage not your worth too
    much:
You are full of quality and fair desert:
Choose of my men which shall attend on you,
And he is yours.   I will allow you, sir,
Your man, your gelding, and your table, all
At my own charge; be my companion.

    Wen. Master Frankford, I have oft been
    bound to you
By many favours; this exceeds them all,
That I shall never merit your least favour:
But, when your last remembrance I forget,
Heaven at my soul exact that weighty debt!

    Frank. There needs no protestation; for I
    know you
Virtuous, and therefore grateful.   Prythee, Nan,
Use him with all thy loving'st courtesy.

    Anne. As far as modesty may well extend,
It is my duty to receive your friend.

    Frank. To dinner, come, sir; from this present
    day,
Welcome to me for ever: come, away.   [*Exit.*

    Nic. I do not like this fellow by no means:
I never see him but my heart still yearns:
Zounds!   I could fight with him, yet know not
    why:
The devil and he are all one in my eye.

                Enter JENKIN.

    Jen. O Nick, what gentleman is that comes

3

to lie at our house?   My master allows him one
to wait on him, and I believe it will fall to thy
lot.

Nic. I love my master; by these hilts I do!
But rather than I'll ever come to serve him,
I'll turn away my master.

Enter CICELY.

Cicely. Nichlas, where are you, Nichlas? you
must come in, Nichlas, and help the young gentleman off with his boots.

Nic. If I pluck off his boots, I'll eat the spurs,
And they shall stick fast in my throat like burs.

Cicely. Then, Jenkin, come you.

Jen. Nay, 'tis no boot for me to deny it.   My
master hath given me a coat here, but he takes
pains himself to brush it once or twice a day
with a holly-wand.

Cicely. Come, come, make haste, that you may
wash your hands again, and help to serve in
dinner.

Jen. You may see, my masters, though it be
afternoon with you, 'tis but early days with us,
for we have not dined yet: stay but a little, I'll
but go in and help to bear up the first course,
and come to you again presently.   [*Exit.*

Enter MALBY *and* CRANWELL.

Mal. This is the sessions-day; pray can you
    tell me
How young Sir Charles hath sped?   Is he acquit,
Or must he try the law's strict penalty?

Cran. He's cleared of all, spite of his enemies,
Whose earnest labour was to take his life:
But in this suit of pardon he hath spent

All the revenues that his father left him;
And he is now turned a plain country man,
Reformed in all things. See, sir, here he comes.

Enter Sir CHARLES *and his* Keeper.

Keep. Discharge your fees. and you are then
  at freedom.
Sir Char. Here, Master Keeper, take the poor
  remainder
Of all the wealth I have: my heavy foes
Have made my purse light; but, alas! to me
'Tis wealth enough that you have set me free.
Mal. God give you joy of your delivery!
I am glad to see you abroad, Sir Charles.
Sir Char. The poorest knight in England,
  Master Malby:
My life hath cost me all my patrimony
My father left his son: well, God forgive them
That are the authors of my penury.

Enter SHAFTON.

Shaf. Sir Charles! a hand, a hand! at liberty?
Now, by the faith I owe, I am glad to see it.
What want you? wherein may I pleasure you?
Sir Char. O me! O most unhappy gentleman!
I am not worthy to have friends stirred up,
Whose hands may help me in this plunge of want.
I would I were in Heaven, to inherit there
The immortal birth-right which my Saviour
  keeps,
And by no unthrift can be bought and sold;
For here on earth what pleasures should we
  trust?
Shaf. To rid you from these contemplations,
Three hundred pounds you shall receive of me;

Nay, five for fail.   Come, sir; the sight of gold
Is the most sweet receipt for melancholy,
And will revive your spirits.   You shall hold law
With your proud adversaries.   Tush, let Frank
    Acton
Wage with his knighthood like expense with me,
And he will sink, he will.   Nay, good Sir Charles,
Applaud your fortune, and your fair escape
From all these perils.
    Sir Char. O sir, they have undone me.
Two thousand and five hundred pound a year
My father at his death possessed me of;
All which the envious Acton made me spend.
And, notwithstanding all this large expense,
I had much ado to gain my liberty:
And I have only now a house of pleasure,
With some five hundred pounds, reserved
Both to maintain me and my loving sister.
    Shaft. [*Aside.*] That must I have, it lies con-
    venient for me:
If I can fasten but one finger on him,
With my full hand I'll gripe him to the heart.
'Tis not for love I proffered him this coin,
But for my gain and pleasure. [*Aloud.*] Come, Sir
    Charles,
I know you have need of money; take my offer.
    Sir Char. Sir, I accept it, and remain indebted
Even to the best of my unable power.
Come, gentlemen, and see it tendered down.
                                            [*Exeunt.*

        Enter WENDOLL *melancholy.*

    Wen. I am a villain if I apprehend
But such a thought: then, to attempt the deed,—
Slave, thou art damned without redemption.
I'll drive away this passion with a song.

A song! ha, ha: a song! as if, fond man,
Thy eyes could swim in laughter, when thy soul
Lies drenched and drownèd in red tears of blood.
I'll pray, and see if God within my heart
Plant better thoughts. Why, prayers are medi-
    tations;
And when I meditate (O God, forgive me!)
It is on her divine perfections.
I will forget her; I will arm myself
Not to entertain a thought of love to her:
And, when I come by chance into her presence,
I'll hale these balls until my eye-strings crack,
From being pulled and drawn to look that way.

Enter over the stage, FRANKFORD, *his Wife, and*
NICHOLAS.

O God! O God! with what a violence
I'm hurried to mine own destruction.
There goest thou, the most perfectest man
That ever England bred a gentleman;
And shall I wrong his bed? Thou God of
    thunder!
Stay in thy thoughts of vengeance and of wrath,
Thy great, almighty, and all-judging hand
From speedy execution on a villain—
A villain, and a traitor to his friend.

Enter JENKIN.

Jenk. Did your worship call?
Wen. He doth maintain me, he allows me
    largely
Money to spend.
Jenk. By my faith, so do not you me; I cannot
get a cross of you.
Wen. My gelding, and my man——

Jenk. That's Sorrell and I.

Wen. This kindness grows of no alliance 'twixt
us——

Jenk. Nor is my service of any great acquaintance.

Wen. I never bound him to me by desert :
Of a mere stranger, a poor gentleman,
A man by whom in no kind he could gain,
He hath placed me in the height of all his
    thoughts,
Made me companion with the best and chiefest
In Yorkshire. He cannot eat without me,
Nor laugh without me : I am to his body
As necessary as his digestion ;
And equally do make him whole or sick :
And shall I wrong this man? Base man ! ingrate !
Hast thou the power straight with thy gory hands
To rip thy image from his bleeding heart?
To scratch thy name from out the holy book
Of his remembrance ; and to wound his name
That holds thy name so dear? Or rend his heart
To whom thy heart was knit and joined together?
And yet I must. Then, Wendoll, be content ;
Thus villains, when they would, cannot repent.

Jenk. What a strange humour is my new
master in ! Pray God he be not mad : if he
should be so, I should never have any mind to
serve him in Bedlam. It may be he's mad for
missing of me.

Wen. What, Jenkin, where's your mistress?

Jenk. Is your worship married?

Wen. Why dost thou ask?

Jenk. Because you are my master ; and if I
have a mistress, I would be glad, like a good
servant, to do my duty to her.

Wen. I mean where's Mistress Frankford.

Jenk. Marry, sir, her husband is riding out of

town, and she went very lovingly to bring him on
his way to horse. Do you see, sir? here she
comes, and here I go.
    Wen. Vanish.   [*Exit* JENKIN.

       Enter Mistress FRANKFORD.

    Anne. You are well met, sir; now, in troth,
      my husband,
Before he took horse, had a great desire
To speak with you : we sought about the house,
Hollaed into the fields, sent every way, ·
But could not meet you : therefore he enjoined me
To do unto you his most kind commends.
Nay, more; he wills you, as you prize his love,
Or hold in estimation his kind friendship,
To make bold in his absence, and command
Even as himself were present in the house :
For you must keep his table, use his servants,
And be a present Frankford in his absence.
    Wen. I thank him for his love.—
[*Aside*] Give me a name, you whose infectious
      tongues
Are tipped with gall and poison; as you would
Think on a man that had your father slain,
Murdered your children, made your wives base
      strumpets,
So call me, call me so. Print in my face
The most stigmatic title of a villain,
For hatching treason to so true a friend.
    Anne. Sir, you are much beholding to my
      husband;
You are a man most dear in his regard.
    Wen. [*Aside.*] I am bound unto your husband,
      and you too.
I will not speak to wrong a gentleman
Of that good estimation, my kind friend :

I will not; zounds! I will not. I may choose,
And I will choose. Shall I be so misled?
Or shall I purchase to my father's crest
The motto of a villain? If I say
I will not do it, what thing can enforce me?
What can compel me? What sad destiny
Hath such command upon my yielding thoughts?
I will not—Ha! some fury pricks me on,
The swift Fates drag me at their chariot-wheel,
And hurry me to mischief. Speak I must;
Injure myself, wrong her, deceive his trust.

    Anne. Are you not well, sir, that you seem thus
      troubled?
There is sedition in your countenance.

    Wen. And in my heart, fair angel, chaste and
      wise.
I love you: start not, speak not, answer not.
I love you: nay, let me speak the rest:
Bid me to swear, and I will call to record
The host of Heaven.

    Anne. The host of Heaven forbid
Wendoll should hatch such a disloyal thought!

    Wen. Such is my fate; to this suit I was born,
To wear rich pleasure's crown, or fortune's scorn.

    Anne. My husband loves you.

    Wen. I know it.

    Anne. He esteems you
Even as his brain, his eye-ball, or his heart.

    Wen. I have tried it.

    Anne. His purse is your exchequer, and his
      table
Doth freely serve you.

    Wen. So I have found it.

    Anne. Oh! with what face of brass, what brow
      of steel,
Can you, unblushing, speak this to the face
Of the espoused wife of so dear a friend?

It is my husband that maintains your state;
Will you dishonour him that in your power
Hath left his whole affairs?   I am his wife,
It is to me you speak.
   Wen. O speak no more!
For more than this I know, and have recorded
Within the red-leaved table of my heart.
Fair, and of all beloved, I was not fearful
Bluntly to give my life into your hand,
And at one hazard all my earthly means.
Go, tell your husband; he will turn me off,
And I am then undone.   I care not, I;
'Twas for your sake.   Perchance in rage he'll kill
   me:
I care not, 'twas for you.   Say I incur
The general name of villain through the world
Of traitor to my friend; I care not, I.
Beggary, shame, death, scandal, and reproach,
For you I'll hazard all: why, what care I?
For you I'll live, and in your love I'll die.
   Anne. You move me, sir, to passion and to
   pity:
The love I bear my husband is as precious
As my soul's health.
   Wen. I love your husband too,
And for his love I will engage my life:
Mistake me not, the augmentation
Of my sincere affection borne to you
Doth no whit lessen my regard of him.
I will be secret, lady, close as night;
And not the light of one small glorious star
Shall shine here in my forehead, to bewray
That act of night.
   Anne. What shall I say?
My soul is wandering, and hath lost her way.
Oh, Master Wendoll! Oh!
   Wen. Sigh not, sweet saint;

For every sigh you breathe draws from my heart
A drop of blood.
   Anne. I ne'er offended yet :
My fault, I fear, will in my brow be writ.
Women that fall, not quite bereft of grace,
Have their offences noted in their face.
I blush and am ashamed.   Oh, Master Wendoll,
Pray God I be not born to curse your tongue,
That hath enchanted me !   This maze I am in
I fear will prove the labyrinth of sin.

Enter NICHOLAS.

   Wen. The path of pleasure, and the gate to
     liss,
Which on your lips I knock at with a kiss.
   Nic. I'll kill the rogue.
   Wen. Your husband is from home, your bed's
     no blab.
Nay, look not down and blush.
   Nic. Zounds ! I'll stab.
Ay, Nick, was it thy chance to come just in the
    nick ?
I love my master, and I hate that slave :
I love my mistress, but these tricks I like not.
My master shall not pocket up this wrong ;
I'll eat my fingers first., Whay say'st thou,
    mettle ?
Does not the rascal Wendoll go on legs
That thou must cut off ?   Hath he not ham-
    strings
That thou must hough ?   Nav. mettle, thou shalt
    stand
To all I say.   I'll henceforth turn a spy,
And watch them in their close conveyances.
I never looked for better of that rascal,
Since he came miching[10] first into our house :

   [10] Entering secretly.

It is that Satan hath corrupted her,
For she was fair and chaste. I'll have an eye
In all their gestures. Thus I think of them,
If they proceed as they have done before:
Wendoll's a knave, my mistress is a——   [*Exit.*

Enter Sir CHARLES MOUNTFORD *and* SUSAN.

Sir Char. Sister, you see we are driven to hard
    shift
To keep this poor house we have left unsold;
I am now enforced to follow husbandry,
And you to milk; and do we not live well?
Well, I thank God.
Susan. O brother, here's a change,
Since old Sir Charles died, in our father's house!
Sir Char. All things on earth thus change,
    some up, some down;
Content's a kingdom, and I wear that crown.

Enter SHAFTON *with a* Serjeant.

Shaf. Good   morrow,   good   morrow,   Sir
    Charles. What, with your sister,
Plying your husbandry? Serjeant, stand off.
You have a pretty house here, and a garden,
And goodly ground about it. Since it lies
So near a lordship that I lately bought,
I would fain buy it of you. I will give you——
Sir Char. O, pardon me: this house succes-
    sively
Hath 'longed to me and my progenitors
Three   hundred   years. My   great-great-grand-
    father,
He in whom first our gentle style began,

Dwelt here; and in this ground, increased this
    mole-hill   '
Unto that mountain which my father left me.
Where he the first of all our house began,
I now the last will end, and keep this house,
This virgin title never yet deflowered
By any unthrift of the Mountfords' line.
In brief, I will not sell it for more gold
Than you could hide or pave the ground withal.
    Shaf. Ha, ha! a proud mind and a beggar's
        purse!
Where's my three hundred pounds, besides the
    use?
I have brought it to an execution
By course of law: what, is my money ready?
    Sir Char. An execution, sir, and never tell me
You put my bond in suit! you deal extremely.
    Shaf. Sell me the land, and I'll acquit you
        straight.
    Sir Char. Alas, alas! 'tis all trouble hath left
        me
To cherish me and my poor sister's life.
If this were sold, our names should then be quite
Razed from the bead-roll of gentility.
You see what hard shift we have made to keep it
Allied still to our own name.   This palm, you see,
Labour hath glowed within; her silver brow,
That never tasted a rough winter's blast
Without a mask or fan, doth with a grace
Defy cold winter, and his storms outface.
    Susan. Sir, we feed sparing, and we labour
        hard,
We lie uneasy, to reserve to us
And our succession this small plot of ground.
    Sir Char. I have so bent my thoughts to hus-
        bandry,
That I protest I scarcely can remember

What a new fashion is; how silk or satin
Feels in my hand : why, pride is grown to us
A mere, mere stranger.   I have quite forgot
The names of all that ever waited on me;
I cannot name ye any of my hounds,
Once from whose echoing mouths I heard all
    music
That e'er my heart desired.   What should I
    say?
To keep this place I have changed myself away.
   Shaf. [*To the* Sergeant.]   Arrest him at my
    suit.   Action and actions
Shall keep thee in continual bondage fast.
Nay, more, I'll sue thee by a late appeal,
And call thy former life in question.
The keeper is my friend, thou shalt have irons,
And usage such as I'll deny to dogs :
Away with him !
   Sir Char. [*To* SUSAN.]   You are too timorous :
But trouble is my master,
And I will serve him truly.—My kind sister,
Thy tears are of no force to mollify
This flinty man.   Go to my father's brother,
My kinsmen and allies; entreat them for me,
To ransom me from this injurious man,
That seeks my ruin.
   Shaf. Come, irons, irons ! come away;
I'll see thee lodged far from the sight of day.
                          [*Exeunt.*
   Susan. My heart's so hardened with the frost
    of grief,
Death cannot pierce it through.   Tyrant too fell !
So lead the fiends condemnèd souls to hell.

      Enter ACTON *and* MALBY.

   Sir Fran. Again to prison !   Malby, hast thou
    seen

A poor slave better tortured? Shall we hear
The music of his voice cry from the grate,
"*Meat for the Lord's sake?*" No, no, yet I
   am not
Throughly revenged. They say he hath a pretty
   wench
Unto his sister: shall I, in mercy-sake
To him and to his kindred, bribe the fool
To shame herself by lewd dishonest lust?
I'll proffer largely; but, the deed being done,
I'll smile to see her base confusion.
   Mal. Methinks, Sir Francis, you are full re-
   venged
For greater wrongs than he can proffer you.
See where the poor sad gentlewoman stands.
   Sir Fran. Ha, ha! now will I flout her poverty,
Deride her fortunes, scoff her base estate;
My very soul the name of Mountford hates.
But stay, my heart! oh, what a look did fly
To strike my soul through with thy piercing eye!
I am enchanted; all my spirits are fled,
And with one glance my envious spleen struck
   dead.
   Susan. Acton! that seeks our blood.
                           [*Runs away.*
   Sir Fran. O chaste and fair!
   Mal. Sir Francis, why, Sir Francis, zounds!
   in a trance?
Sir Francis, what cheer, man? Come, come,
   how is't?
   Sir Fran. Was she not fair? Or else this
   judging eye
Cannot distinguish beauty.
   Mal. She was fair.
   Sir Fran. She was an angel in a mortal's
   shape,
And ne'er descended from old Mountford's line.

But soft, soft, let me call my wits together.
A poor, poor wench, to my great adversary
Sister, whose very souls denounce stern war,
One against other. How now, Frank? turned
    fool
Or madman, whether? But no; master of
My perfect senses and directest wits.
Then why should I be in this violent humour
Of passion and of love? And with a person
So different every way, and so opposed
In all contractions, and still-warring actions?
Fie, fie; how I dispute against my soul!
Come, come; I'll gain her, or in her fair quest
Purchase my soul free and immortal rest.
                        [Exeunt.

Enter Three or Four Serving-Men, *one with a
    voider and a wooden knife to take away all;
    another with the salt and bread; another with
    the table-cloth and napkins; another with the
    carpet:* JENKIN *with two lights after them.*

Jenk. So, march in order, and retire in battle
array. My master and the guests have supped
already, all's taken away: here, now spread for
the serving-men in the hall. Butler, it belongs
to your office.
    But. I know it, Jenkin. What d'ye call the
gentleman that supped there to-night?
    Jenk. Who, my master?
    But. No, no; Master Wendoll, he's a daily
guest: I mean the gentleman that came but this
afternoon.
    Jenk. His name's Master Cranwell. God's
light, hark, within there, my master calls to lay
more billets upon the fire. Come, come! Lord,

how we that are in office here in the house are
troubled! One spread the carpet in the parlour,
and stand ready to snuff the lights; the rest be
ready to prepare their stomachs.   More lights
in the hall there.   Come, Nicholas.   [*Exit.*
   Nic. I cannot eat, but had I Wendoll's heart
I would eat that; the rogue grows impudent.
Oh, I have seen such vile notorious tricks,
Ready to make my eyes dart from my head.
I'll tell my master, by this air I will!
Fall what may fall, I'll tell him.   Here he comes.

Enter Master FRANKFORD, *brushing the crumbs
    from his clothes with a napkin, as newly
    risen from supper.*

   Frank. Nicholas, what make you here? why
    are not you
At supper in the hall among your fellows?
   Nic. Master, I stayed your rising from the
    board,
To speak with you.
   Frank. Be brief, then, gentle Nicholas;
My wife and guests attend me in the parlour.
Why dost thou pause?   Now, Nicholas, you
    want money,
And, unthrift-like, would eat into your wages
Ere you have earned it: here, sir,'s half a
    crown;
Play the good husband,[11] and away to supper.
   Nic. By this hand, an honourable gentleman!
I will not see him wronged.—Sir, I have served
you long; you entertained me seven years before
your beard.   You knew me, sir, before you knew
my mistress.

   11 In the sense of husbandry.

Frank. What of this, good Nicholas?

Nic. I never was a make-bate[12] or a knave;
I have no fault but one: I'm given to quarrel,
But not with women. I will tell you, master,
That which will make your heart leap from your
    breast,
Your hair to startle from your head, your ears
    to tingle.

Frank. What preparation's this to dismal
    news?

Nic. 'Sblood, sir! I love you better than
    your wife;
I'll make it good.

Frank. You are a knave, and I have much
    ado
With wonted patience to contain my rage,
And not to break thy pate. Thou art a knave:
I'll turn you, with your base comparisons,
Out of my doors.

Nic. Do, do:
There is not room for Wendoll and for me
Both in one house. Oh master, master!
That Wendoll is a villain.

Frank. Ay, saucy!

Nic. Strike, strike; do, strike; yet hear me:
    I am no fool,
I know a villain, when I see him act
Deeds of a villain. Master, master, that base
    slave
Enjoys my mistress, and dishonours you.

Frank. Thou hast killed me with a weapon
    whose sharp point
Hath pricked quite through and through my
    shivering heart:
Drops of cold sweat sit dangling on my hairs,

---

[12] A quarrelsome person.

4

Like morning's dew upon the golden flowers,
And I am plunged into strange agonies.
What didst thou say? If any word that touched
His credit or her reputation,
It is as hard to enter my belief
As Dives into heaven.

   Nic. I can gain nothing;
They are two that never wronged me. I knew
    before
'Twas but a thankless office, and perhaps
As much as is my service, or my life
Is worth. All this I know; but this and more,
More by a thousand dangers, could not hire me
To smother such a heinous wrong from you.
I saw, and I have said.

   Frank. [*Aside.*] 'Tis probable; though blunt,
    yet he is honest:
Though I durst pawn my life, and on their faith
Hazard the dear salvation of my soul,
Yet in my trust I may be too secure.
May this be true? O, may it? Can it be?
Is it by any wonder possible?
Man, woman, what thing mortal may we trust,
When friends and bosom wives prove so un-
    just?—
[*To* Nicholas.] What instance hast thou of this
    strange report?

   Nic. Eyes, eyes.

   Frank. Thy eyes may be deceived, I tell thee:
For, should an angel from the heavens drop
    down,
And preach this to me that thyself hast told,
He should have much ado to win belief;
In both their loves I am so confident.

   Nic. Shall I discourse the same by circum-
    stance?

Frank. No more! to supper, and command
  your fellows
To attend us and the strangers. Not a word,
I charge thee on thy life: be secret then,
For I know nothing.
  Nic. I am dumb; and, now that I have eased
  my stomach,
I will go fill my stomach.
  Frank. Away; be gone.
She is well born, descended nobly;
Virtuous her education, her repute
Is in the general voice of all the country
Honest and fair; her carriage, her demeanour,
In all her actions that concern the love
To me her husband, modest, chaste, and godly.
Is all this seeming gold plain copper?
But he, that Judas that hath borne my purse,
And sold me for a sin!—Oh God! Oh God!
Shall I put up these wrongs? No. Shall I trust
The bare report of this suspicious groom,
Before the double-gilt, the well-hatched ore
Of their two hearts? No, I will lose these
  thoughts:
Distraction I will banish from my brow,
And from my looks exile sad discontent,
Their wonted favours in my tongue shall flow;
Till I know all, I'll nothing seem to know.
Lights and a table there! Wife, Master Wen-
  doll,
And gentle Master Cranwell.

Enter Mistress FRANKFORD, WENDOLL, CRAN-
  WELL, NICHOLAS, *and* JENKIN, *with cards,
  carpet, stools, and other necessaries.*

  Frank. O Master Cranwell, you are a stranger
  here,

And often baulk my house: faith, y'are a churl.
Now we have supped, a table, and to cards.

Jenk. A pair of cards,[13] Nicholas, and a carpet to cover the table.   Where's Cicely with her
counters and her box?   Candles and candlesticks
there! Fie, we have such a household of serving
creatures! unless it be Nick and I, there's not
one amongst them all can say bo to a goose.
Well said, Nick.

[*They spread a carpet, set down lights and cards.*

Anne. Come, Master Frankford, who shall
    take my part?

Frank. Marry, that will I, sweet wife.

Wen. No, by my faith, sir; when you are
together I sit out: it must be Mistress Frankford
and I, or else it is no match.

Frank. I do not like that match.

Nic. [*Aside.*] You have no reason, marry,
    knowing all.

Frank. 'Tis no great matter neither.   Come,
Master Cranwell, shall you and I take them up?

Cran. At your pleasure, sir.

Frank. I must look to you, Master Wendoll,
for you will be playing false; nay, so will my
wife too.

Nic. [*Aside.*] Ay, I will be sworn she will.

Anne. Let them that are taken playing false,
forfeit the set.

Frank. Content; it shall go hard but I'll take
you.

Cran. Gentlemen, what shall our game be?

Wen. Master Frankford, you play best at
" noddy."

Frank. You shall not find it so; indeed you
shall not.

13 A pack.

Anne. I can play at nothing so well as " double ruff."

Frank. If Master Wendoll and my wife be together, there's no playing against them at double hand.

Nic. I can tell you, sir, the game that Master Wendoll is best at.

Wen. What game is that, Nick?

Nic. Marry, sir, " Knave out of Doors."

Wen. She and I will take you at " Lodam."

Anne. Husband, shall we play at " Saint?"

Frank. My saint's turned devil.   No, we'll none of " Saint:"
You are best at " New-cut," wife; you'll play
    at that.

Wen. If you play at " New-cut," I am soonest hitter of any here, for a wager.

Frank. 'Tis me they play on. Well, you may
    draw out.
For all your cunning, 'twill be to your shame;
I'll teach you, at your " New-cut," a new game.
Come, come.

Cran. If you cannot agree upon the game, to post and pair.

Wen. We shall be soonest pairs; and my good
    host,
When he comes late home, he must kiss the
    post.

Frank. Whoever wins, it shall be to thy cost.

Cran. Faith, let it be " Vide-ruff," and let's make honours.

Frank. If you make honours, one thing let
    me crave :
Honour the king and queen; except the knave.

Wen. Well, as you please for that. Lift who shall deal.

Anne. The least in sight: what are you,
Master Wendoll?

Wen. I am a knave.

Nic. [*Aside.*] I'll swear it.

Anne. I a queen.

Frank. [*Aside.*] A quean thou shouldst say.
  [*Aloud*]. Well, the cards are mine;
They are the grossest pair that e'er I felt.

Anne. Shuffle, I'll cut: would I had never
dealt.

Frank. I have lost my dealing.

Wen. Sir, the fault's in me:
This queen I have more than mine own, you see.
Give me the stock.

Frank. My mind's not on my game.
Many a deal I have lost; the more's your shame.
You have served me a bad trick, Master Wendoll.

Wen. Sir, you must take your lot.   To end
   this strife,
I know I have dealt better with your wife.

Frank. Thou hast dealt falsely, then.

Anne. What's trumps?

Wen. Hearts: partner, I rub.

Frank. [*Aside.*] Thou robb'st me of my soul,
   of her chaste love;
In thy false dealing thou hast robbed my heart.
[*Aloud.*] Booty you play; I like a loser stand,
Having no heart, or here or in my hand.
I will give o'er the set; I am not well.
Come, who will hold my cards ?

Anne. Not well,' sweet Master Frankford!
Alas, what ail you? 'Tis some sudden qualm.

Wen. How long have you been so, Master
   Frankford?

Frank. Sir, I was lusty, and I had my health,
But I grew ill when you began to deal.
Take hence this table. Gentle Master Cranwell,

You are welcome; see your chamber at your
 pleasure.
I'm sorry that this meagrim takes me so,
I cannot sit and bear you company.
Jenkin, some lights, and show him to his
 chamber.
 Anne. A night-gown for my husband; quickly
 there:
It is some rheum or cold.
 Wen. Now, in good faith, this illness you
 have got
By sitting late without your gown.
 Frank. I know it, Master Wendoll.
Go, go to bed, lest you complain like me.
Wife, prythee, wife, into my bed-chamber;
The night is raw and cold, and rheumatic:
Leave me my gown and light; I'll walk away
 my fit.
 Wen. Sweet sir, good night.
 Frank. Myself, good night. [*Exit* WENDOLL.
 Anne. Shall I attend you, husband?
 Frank. No, gentle wife, thou'lt catch cold in
 thy head;
Prythee, be gone, sweet; I'll make haste to bed.
 Anne. No sleep will fasten on mine eyes, you
 know,
Until you come.
 Frank. Sweet Nan, I prythee go.—
                    [*Exit* Mistress FRANKFORD.
I have bethought me: get me, by degrees,
The keys of all my doors, which I will mould
In wax, and take their fair impression,
To have by them new keys. This being com-
 passed,
At a set hour a letter shall be brought me,
And, when they think they may securely play,
They are nearest to danger. Nick, I must rely

You know me, Master Sandy, and my suit.
   Sandy. I knew you, lady, when the old man
    lived;
I knew you ere your brother sold his land;
Then you sung well, played sweetly on the lute;
But now I neither know you nor your suit.
   Susan. You, Master Roder, was my brother's
    tenant,
Rent-free he placed you in that wealthy farm,
Of which you are possessed. ·
   Roder. True, he did;
And have I not there dwelt still for his sake?
I have some business now; but, without doubt,
They that have hurled him in will help him out.
   Susan. Cold comfort still : what say you, cousin
    Tidy?
   Tidy. I say this comes of roysting, swagger-
    ing.
Call me not cousin : each man for himself.
Some men are born to mirth, and some to sorrow,
I am no cousin unto them that borrow.　　[*Exit.*
   Susan. O charity ! why art thou fled to heaven,
And left all things upon this earth uneven?
Their scoffing answers I will ne'er return;
But to myself his grief in silence mourn.

    Enter Sir Francis *and* Malby.

   Sir Fran. She is poor, I'll therefore tempt her
    with this gold.
Go, Malby, in my name deliver it,
And I will stay thy answer.
   Malby. Fair mistress, as I understand, your
    grief
Doth grow from want, so I have here in store
A means to furnish you, a bag of gold,
Which to your hands I freely tender you.

Susan. I thank you, Heavens! I thank you,
    gentle sir:
God make me able to requite this favour!

Mal. This gold Sir Francis Acton sends by me,
And prays you——

Susan. Acton! O God! that name I am born
    to curse:
Hence, bawd! hence, broker! see, I spurn his
    gold;
My honour never shall for gain be sold.

Sir Fran. Stay, lady, stay.

Susan. From you I'll posting hie,
Even as the doves from feathered eagles fly.
                                        [*Exit.*

Sir Fran. She hates my name, my face: how
    should I woo?
I am disgraced in everything I do.
The more she hates me, and disdains my love,
The more I am rapt in admiration
Of her divine and chaste perfections.
Woo her with gifts I cannot, for all gifts
Sent in my name she spurns.   With looks I
    cannot,
For she abhors my sight.   Not yet with letters,
For none she will receive.   How then, how then?
Well, I will fasten such a kindness on her
As shall o'ercome her hate and conquer it.
Sir Charles, her brother, lies in execution
For a great sum of money; and, besides,
The appeal is sued still for my huntsman's death,
Which only I have power to reverse:
In her I'll bury all my hate of him.
Go seek the keeper, Malby, bring him to me:
To save his body, I his debts will pay;
To save his life, I his appeal will stay. [*Exeunt.*

Enter Sir CHARLES MOUNTFORD *in prison with irons, his feet bare, his garments all ragged and torn.*

Sir Char. Of all on the earth's face most miserable,
Breathe in this hellish dungeon thy laments,
Thus like a slave ragged, like a felon gyved.
What hurls thee headlong to this base estate?
O unkind uncle! O my friends ingrate!
Unthankful kinsmen! Mountford's all too base,
To let thy name be fettered in disgrace!
A thousand deaths here in this grave I die;
Fear, hunger, sorrow, cold, all threat my death,
And join together to deprive my breath.
But that which most torments me, my dear sister
Hath left to visit me, and from my friends
Hath brought no hopeful answer: therefore I
Divine they will not help my misery.
If it be so, shame, scandal, and contempt
Attend their covetous thoughts. Need make their graves!
Usurers they live, and may they die like slaves!

Enter Keeper.

Keep. Knight, be of comfort, for I bring thee freedom
From all thy troubles.
Sir Char. Then I am doomed to die;
Death is the end of all calamity.
Keep. Live: your appeal is stayed; the execution
Of all your debts discharged; your creditors
Even to the utmost penny satisfied,
In sign whereof, your shackles I knock off;
You are not left so much indebted to us

Susan. Charles, can you mock me in your
   poverty,
Knowing your friends deride your misery?
Now, I protest I stand so much amazed
To see your bonds free, and your irons knocked
   off,
That I am rapt into a maze of wonder:
The rather for I know not by what means
This happiness hath chanced.
   Sir Char. Why, by my uncle,
My cousins, and my friends: who else, I pray,
Would take upon them all my debts to pay?
   Susan. O brother, they are men all of flint,
Pictures of marble, and as void of pity
As chased bears. I begged, I sued, I kneeled,
Laid open all your griefs and miseries,
Which they derided; more than that, denied us
A part in their alliance; but, in pride,
Said that our kindred with our plenty died.
   Sir Char. Drudges too much, what did they:
   oh, known evil!
Rich fly the poor, as good men shun the devil.
Whence should my freedom come? of whom
   alive,
Saving of those, have I deserved so well?
Guess, sister, call to mind, remember me:
These I have raised, they follow the world's
   guise;
Whom rich in honour, they in woe despise.
   Susan. My wits have lost themselves, let's ask
   the keeper.
   Sir Char. Gaoler!
   Keep. At hand, sir.
   Sir Char. Of courtesy resolve me one demand.
What was he took the burthen· of my debts
From off my back, stayed my appeal to death,
Discharged my fees, and brought me liberty?

From them this action had deserved my life:
And from a stranger more; because from such
There is less execution of good deeds.
But he, nor father, nor ally, nor friend,
More than a stranger, both remote in blood
And in his heart opposed my enemy,—
That this high bounty should proceed from
    him,—
Oh, there I lose myself! What should I say,
What think, what do, his bounty to repay?
    Susan. You, wonder, I am sure, whence this
      strange kindness
Proceeds in Acton. I will tell you, brother:
He dotes on me, and oft hath sent me gifts,
Letters and tokens. I refused them all.
    Sir Char. I have enough, though poor; my
      heart is set,
In one rich gift to pay back all my debt.
                           [Exeunt.

Enter FRANKFORD, *and* NICHOLAS *with keys, and
a letter in his hand.*

    Frank. This is the night that I must play my
      part
To try two seeming angels. Where's my keys?
    Nic. They are made according to your mould
      in wax:
I bade the smith be secret, gave him money,
And here they are. The letter, sir.
    Frank. True, take it, there it is;
And when thou seest me in my pleasant'st vein,
Ready to sit to supper, bring it me.
    Nic. I'll do't, make no more question but I'll
      do't.   *[Exit.*

Enter Mistress FRANKFORD, CRANWELL, WEN-
DOLL, *and* JENKIN.

Anne. Sirrah, 'tis six o'clock already struck!
Go bid them spread the cloth and serve in supper.
Jenk. It shall be done, forsooth, mistress.
Where's Spigot, the butler, to give us out salt
and trenchers?
Wen. We that have been a-hunting all the day
Come with preparèd stomachs. Master Frank-
    ford,
We wished you at our sport.
Frank. My heart was with you, and my mind
    was on you.
Fie, Master Cranwell! you are still thus sad?
A stool, a stool. Where's Jenkin, and where's
    Nick?
'Tis supper-time at least an hour ago.
What's the best news abroad?
Wen. I know none good.
Frank. [*Aside.*] But I know too much bad.

Enter Butler *and* JENKIN *with a table-cloth, bread,
    trenchers, and salt.*

Cran. Methinks, sir, you might have that in-
    terest
In your wife's brother, to be more remiss
In his hard dealing against poor Sir Charles,
Who, as I hear, lies in York Castle, needy,
And in great want.
Frank. Did not more weighty business of my
    own
Hold me away, I would have laboured peace
Betwixt them, with all care: indeed I would, sir.
Anne. I'll write unto my brother earnestly

In that behalf.

Wen. A charitable deed,
And will beget the good opinion
Of all your friends that love you, Mistress Frank-
ford.

Frank. That's you for one; I know you love
Sir Charles,
And my wife too, well.

Wen. He deserves the love
Of all true gentlemen; be yourselves judge.

Frank. But supper, ho! Now as thou lov'st
me, Wendoll,
Which I am sure thou dost, be merry, pleasant,
And frolic it to-night. Sweet Master Cranwell,
Do you the like. Wife, I protest my heart
Was ne'er more bent on sweet alacrity.
Where be those lazy knaves to serve in supper?

Enter NICHOLAS.

Nic. Here's a letter, sir.

Frank. Whence comes it? and who brought it?

Nic. A stripling that below attends your
answer,
And, as he tells me, it is sent from York.

Frank. Have him into the cellar; let him taste
A cup of our March beer: go, make him drink.

Nic. I'll make him drunk, if he be a Trojan.

Frank. [*Reads the letter.*]   My boots and
spurs! where's Jenkin? God forgive me,
How I neglect my business! Wife, look here;
I have a matter to be tried to-morrow
By eight o'clock, and my attorney writes me,
I must be there betimes with evidence,
Or it will go against me. Where's my boots?

5

Enter JENKIN *with boots and spurs.*

Anne. I hope your business craves no such despatch
That you must ride to-night.
Wen. [*Aside.*] I hope it doth.
Frank. God's me! no such despatch!
Jenkin, my boots. Where's Nick? Saddle my
    roan,
And the grey dapple for himself. Content ye,
It much concerns me. Gentle Master Cranwell,
And Master Wendoll, in my absence use
The very ripest pleasures of my house.
Wen. Lord! Master Frankford, will you ride
    to-night?
The ways are dangerous.
Frank. Therefore will I ride
Appointed well; and so shall Nick my man.
Anne. I'll call you up by five o'clock to-
    morrow.
Frank. No, by my faith, wife, I'll not trust
    to that;
'Tis not such easy rising in a morning
From one I love so dearly. No, by my faith,
I shall not leave so sweet a bedfellow,
But with much pain. You have made me a slug-
    gard
Since I first knew you.
Anne. Then, if you needs will go
This dangerous evening, Master Wendoll,
Let me entreat you bear him company.
Wen. With all my heart, sweet mistress. My
    boots there!
Frank. Fie, fie, that for my private business
I should disease[15] my friend, and be a trouble

15 Dis-ease.

To the whole house! Nick!

  Nic. Anon, sir.

  Frank. Bring forth my gelding.—As you love
   me sir,

Use no more words: a hand, good Master Cranwell.

  Cran. Sir, God be your good speed!

  Frank. Good night, sweet Nan; nay, nay, a
   kiss and part.

[*Aside.*] Dissembling lips, you suit not with my
   heart.   [*Exit.*

  Wen. How business, time, and hours, all
   gracious prove,

And are the furtherers to my new-born love!

I am husband now in Master Frankford's place,

And must command the house. My pleasure is

We will not sup abroad so publicly,

But in your private chamber, Mistress Frankford.

  Anne. O, sir, you are too public in your love,

And Master Frankford's wife.

  Cran. Might I crave favour,

I would entreat you I might see my chamber;

I am on the sudden grown exceeding ill,

And would be spared from supper.

  Wen. Light there, ho!

See you want nothing, sir; for, if you do,

You injure that good man, and wrong me too.

  Cran. I will make bold: good night. [*Exit.*

  Wen. How all conspire

To make our bosom sweet, and full entire!

Come, Nan, I pr'ythee let us sup within.

  Anne. Oh, what a clog unto the soul is sin!

We pale offenders are still full of fear;

Every suspicious eye brings danger near,

When they whose clear hearts from offence are
   free

Despise report, base scandals do outface,

And stand at mere defiance with disgrace.

Wen. Fie, fie! you talk too like a puritan.

Anne. You have tempted me to mischief,
  Master Wendoll:

I have done I know not what. Well, you plead
  custom;

That which for want of wit I granted erst,

I now must yield through fear. Come, come,
  let's in;

Once o'er shoes, we are straight o'er head in sin.

Wen. My jocund soul is joyful above measure;

I'll be profuse in Frankford's richest treasure.

　　　　　　　　　　　　　　　　　　　[Exeunt.

Enter CICELY, JENKIN, *and* Butler.

Jenk. My mistress and Master Wendoll, my
master, sup in her chamber to-night.   Cicely,
you are preferred from being the cook to be
chambermaid.   Of all the loves betwixt thee and
me, tell me what thou thinkest of this?

Cicely. Mum; there's an old proverb,—when
the cat's away, the mouse may play.

Jenk. Now you talk of a cat, Cicely, I smell
a rat.

Cicely. Good words, Jenkin, lest you be called
to answer them.

Jenk. Why, God made my mistress an honest
woman!   Are not these good words?   Pray God
my new master play not the knave with my old
master!   Is there any hurt in this?   God send
no villainy intended! and, if they do sup together,
pray God they do not lie together!   God make
my mistress chaste, and make us all His servants!
what harm is there in all this?   Nay, more; here
is my hand, thou shalt never have my heart unless
thou say Amen.

Cicely. Amen, I pray God, I say.

Enter Serving-man.

Serv. My mistress sends that you should make less noise, to lock up the doors, and see the household all got to bed. You, Jenkin, for this night are made the porter to see the gates shut in.

Jenk. Thus, by little and little, I creep into office. Come, to kennel, my masters, to kennel; 'tis eleven o'clock, already.

Serv. When you have locked the gates in, you must send up the keys to my mistress.

Cicely. Quickly, for God's sake, Jenkin, for I must carry them. I am neither pillow nor bolster, but I know more than both.

Jenk. To bed, good Spigot; to bed, good honest serving-creatures; and let us sleep as snug as pigs in pease-straw.   [*Exeunt.*

Enter FRANKFORD *and* NICHOLAS.

Frank. Soft, soft; we have tied our geldings
　　to a tree,
Two flight-shoot[16] off, lest by their thundering
　　hoofs
They blab our coming back. Hear'st thou no
　　noise?

Nic. Hear! I hear nothing but the owl and
　　you.

Frank. So: now my watch's hand points upon
　　twelve,
And it is dead midnight. Where are my keys?

Nic. Here, sir.

---

[16] The distance a flight-arrow would go—about one-fifth of a mile.

Frank. This is the key that opes my outward
　　gate;
This is the hall-door; this the withdrawing
　　chamber;
But this, that door that's bawd unto my shame,
Fountain and spring of all my bleeding thoughts,
Where the most hallowed order and true knot
Of nuptial sanctity hath been profaned;
It leads to my polluted bed-chamber,
Once my terrestrial heaven, now my earth's hell,
The place where sins in all their ripeness dwell.—
But I forget myself: now to my gate.
　　Nic. It must ope with far less noise than
Cripple-gate, or your plot's dashed.
　　Frank. So, reach me my dark lanthorn to the
　　rest;
Tread softly, softly.
　　Nic. I will walk on eggs this pace.
　　Frank. A general silence hath surprised the
　　house,
And this is the last door. Astonishment,
Fear, and amazement play against my heart,
Even as a madman beats upon a drum.
Oh, keep my eyes, you Heavens, before I enter,
From any sight that may transfix my soul;
Or, if there be so black a spectacle,
Oh, strike mine eyes stark blind; or, if not so,
Lend me such patience to digest my grief
That I may keep this white and virgin hand
From any violent outrage or red murder!
And with that prayer I enter.　　　　　　[*Exit.*
　　Nic. Here's a circumstance.
A man be made cuckold in the time
That he's about it. An the case were mine,
As 'tis my master's,—'sblood that he makes me
　　swear!—
I would have placed his action, entered there;

I would, I would.

Re-enter FRANKFORD.

Frank. Oh! oh!

Nic. Master, 'sblood! master! master!

Frank. O me unhappy! I have found them lying
Close in each other's arms, and fast asleep.
But that I would not damn two precious souls,
Bought with my Saviour's blood, and send them, laden
With all their scarlet sins upon their backs,
Unto a fearful judgment, their two lives
Had met upon my rapier!

Nic. 'Sblood, master. What, have you left
them sleeping still? let me go wake them.

Frank. Stay, let me pause a while.
O God! O God! that it were possible
To undo things done; to call back yesterday!
That time could turn up his swift sandy glass,
To untell the days, and to redeem these hours!
Or that the sun
Could, rising from the west, draw his coach backward,
Take from the account of time so many minutes,
Till he had all these seasons called again,
Those minutes, and those actions done in them,
Even from her first offence; that I might take her
As spotless as an angel in my arms!
But, oh! I talk of things impossible,
And cast beyond the moon. God give me patience!
For I will in and wake them.   [*Exit.*

Nic. Here's patience perforce;
He needs must trot afoot that tires his horse.

Enter WENDOLL, *running over the stage in a*
night-gown, FRANKFORD *after him with a*
sword drawn; a Maid-servant *in her smock*
stays his hand, and clasps hold on him.
FRANKFORD *pauses for a while.*

   Frank. I thank thee, maid; thou, like the
     angel's hand,
Hast stayed me from a bloody sacrifice.
                    [*Exit* Maid-servant.
Go, villain, and my wrongs sit on thy soul
As heavy as this grief doth upon mine!
When thou record'st my many courtesies,
And shalt compare them with thy treacherous
     heart,
Lay them together, weigh them equally,
'Twill be revenge enough. Go, to thy friend
A Judas: pray, pray, lest I live to see
Thee, Judas-like, hanged on an elder-tree,

Enter Mistress FRANKFORD *in her smock, night-*
gown, and night attire.

   Anne. Oh, by what word, what title, or what
     name,
Shall I entreat your pardon? Pardon! oh!
I am as far from hoping such sweet grace
As Lucifer from heaven. To call you husband—
O me, most wretched! I have lost that name,
I am no more your wife.
   Nic. 'Sblood, sir, she swoons.
   Frank. Spare thou thy tears, for I will weep
     for thee:
And keep thy countenance, for I'll blush for thee.
Now, I protest, I think 'tis I am tainted,
For I am most ashamed; and 'tis more hard
For me to look upon thy guilty face,

Than on the sun's clear brow. What would'st
    thou speak?
  Anne. I would I had no tongue, no ears, no
    eyes,
No apprehension, no capacity.
When do you spurn me like a dog? when tread
  me
Under your feet? when drag me by the hair?
Though I deserve a thousand fold
More than you can inflict : yet, once my husband,
For womanhood, to which I am a shame,
Though once an ornament—even for His sake
That hath redeemed our souls, mark not my face
Nor hack me with your sword; but let me go
Perfect and undeformèd to my tomb.
I am not worthy that I should prevail
In the least suit; no, not to speak to you,
Nor look on you, nor to be in your presence.
Yet, as an abject, this one suit I crave;
This granted, I am ready for my grave.   [*Kneels.*
  Frank. My God, with patience arm me! Rise,
    nay, rise,
And I'll debate with thee. Was it for want
Thou playedst the strumpet? Wast thou not
  supplied
With every pleasure, fashion, and new toy;
Nay, even beyond my calling?
  Anne. I was.
  Frank. Was it then disability in me;
Or in thine eye seemed he a properer man?
  Anne. Oh, no.
  Frank. Did not I lodge thee in my bosom?
Wear thee here in my heart?
  Anne. You did.
  Frank. I did, indeed; witness my tears I did.
Go, bring my infants hither.

Two Children *are brought in by* Servant.

O Nan! O Nan!
If neither fear of shame, regard of honour,
The blemish of my house, nor my dear love
Could have withheld thee from so lewd a fact,
Yet for these infants, these young harmless souls,
On whose white brows thy shame is charactered,
And grows in greatness as they wax in years,—
Look but on them, and melt away in tears.
Away with them! lest, as her spotted body
Hath stained their names with stripe of bastardy,
So her adulterous breath may blast their spirits
With her infectious thoughts.   Away with them!
   Anne. In this one life I die ten thousand deaths.
   Frank. Stand up, stand up; I will do nothing
      rashly;
I will retire a while into my study,
And thou shalt hear thy sentence presently.
                                                [*Exit.*

   Anne. 'Tis welcome, be it death.   O me, base
      strumpet,
That, having such a husband, such sweet children,
Must enjoy neither!   Oh, to redeem my honour,
I would have this hand cut off, these my breasts
      seared,
Be racked, strappadoed, put to any torment:
Nay, to whip but this scandal out, I would hazard
The rich and dear redemption of my soul.
He cannot be so base as to forgive me;
Nor I so shameless to accept his pardon.
O women, women, you that yet have kept
Your holy matrimonial vow unstained,
Make me your instance: when you tread awry,
Your sins, like mine, will on your conscience lie.

Enter CICELY, JENKIN, SPIGGOT, *and all the*
serving-men, as newly come out of bed.

All. O mistress, mistress, what have you done,
mistress?

Nic. 'Sblood, what a caterwauling keep you
here !

Jenk. O Lord, mistress, how comes this to
pass?   My master is run away in his shirt,
and never so much as called me to bring his
clothes after him.

Anne. See what guilt is ! Here stand I in
    this place,
Ashamed to look my servants in the face.

Enter FRANKFORD *and* CRANWELL, *whom,*
seeing, she falls on her knees.

Frank. My words are registered in Heaven
    already,
With patience hear me.   I'll not martyr thee,
Nor mark thee for a strumpet; but with usage
Of more humility torment thy soul,
And kill thee even with kindness.
    Cran. Master Frankford !
    Frank. Good Master Cranwell.   Woman, hear
    thy judgment.
Go make thee ready in thy best attire;
Take with thee all thy gowns, all thy apparel;
Leave nothing that did ever call thee mistress,
Or by whose sight, being left here in the house,
I may remember such a woman by.
Choose thee a bed and hangings for thy chamber;
Take with thee every thing that hath thy mark,
And get thee to my manor seven mile off,
Where live; 'tis thine; I freely give it thee.

O sister !——

   Susan. O brother, what doth this strange lan-
      guage mean?

   Sir Char. Dost love me, sister? wouldst thou
      see me live
A bankrupt beggar in the world's disgrace,
And die indebted to my enemies?
Wouldst thou behold me stand like a huge beam
In the world's eye, a bye-word and a scorn?
It lies in thee of these to acquit me free,
And all my debt I may out-strip by thee.

   Susan. By me! why, I have nothing, nothing
      left;
I owe even for the clothes upon my back;
I am not worth——

   Sir Char. O sister, say not so;
It lies in you my downcast state to raise,
To make me stand on even points with the world.
Come, sister, you are rich; indeed you are;
And in your power you have, without delay,
Acton's five hundred pound back to repay.

   Susan. Till now I had thought you had loved
      me. By my honour
(Which I have kept as spotless as the moon), —
I ne'er was mistress of that single doit
Which I reserved not to supply your wants;
And do you think that I would hoard from you?
Now, by my hopes in Heaven, knew I the means
To buy you from the slavery of your debts
(Especially from Acton, whom I hate),
I would redeem it with my life or blood.

   Sir Char. I challenge it; and, kindred set apart,
Thus, ruffian-like, I lay siege to your heart.
What do I owe to Acton?

   Susan. Why some five hundred pounds; to-
      wards which, I swear,

In all the world I have not one denier.[17]

Sir Char. It will not prove so. Sister, now
  resolve me :
What do you think (and speak you conscience)
Would Acton give, might he enjoy your bed?

Susan. He would not shrink to spend a thousand pound,
To give the Mountfords' name so deep a wound.

Sir Char. A thousand pound ! I but five hundred owe ;
Grant him your bed, he's paid with interest so.

Susan. O brother !

Sir Char. O sister ! only this one way,
With that rich jewel you my debts may pay.
In speaking this my cold heart shakes with shame ;
Nor do I woo you in a brother's name,
But in a stranger's. Shall I die in debt
To Acton, my grand foe, and you still wear
The precious jewel that he holds so dear?

Susan. My honour I esteem as dear and
  precious
As my redemption.

Sir Char. I esteem you, sister,
As dear, for so dear prizing it.

Susan. Will Charles
Have me cut off my hands, and send them Acton?
Rip up my breast, and with my bleeding heart
Present him as a token?

Sir Char. Neither, sister :
But hear me in my strange assertion.
Thy honour and my soul are equal in my regard ;
Nor will thy brother Charles survive thy shame.
His kindness, like a burthen hath surcharged me,
And under his good deeds I stooping go,
Not with an upright soul. Had I remained

17 French for a penny

In prison still, there doubtless I had died :
Then, unto him that freed me from that prison,
Still do I owe this life. What moved my foe
To enfranchise me? 'Twas, sister, for your love.
With full five hundred pounds he bought your
    love,
And shall he not enjoy it? Shall the weight
Of all this heavy burthen lean on me,
And will not you bear part? You did partake
The joy of my release; will you not stand
In joint-bond bound to satisfy the debt?
Shall I be only charged?
  Susan. But that I know
These arguments come from an honoured mind,
As in your most extremity of need
Scorning to stand in debt to one you hate,—
Nay, rather would engage your unstained honour
Than to be held ingrate,—I should condemn you.
I see your resolution, and assent;
So Charles will have me, and I am content.
  Sir Char. For this I tricked you up.
  Susan. But here's a knife,
To save mine honour, shall slice out my life.
  Sir Char. Ay! know thou pleasest me a thou-
    sand times
More in that resolution than thy grant.—
Observe her love; to soothe it to my suit,
Her honour she will hazard, though not loose :
To bring me out of debt, her rigorous hand
Will pierce her heart. O wonder! that will
    choose,
Rather than stain her blood, her life to lose.—
Come, you sad sister to a woful brother,
This is the gate : I'll bear him such a present,
Such an acquaintance for the knight to seal,
As will amaze his senses, and surprise
With admiration all his fantasies.

Enter Sir FRANCIS ACTON *and* MALBY.

Susan. Before his unchaste thoughts shall
    seize on me,
'Tis here shall my imprisoned soul set free.
   Sir Fran. How! Mountford with his sister,
    hand in hand!
What miracle's afoot?
   Mal. It is a sight
Begets in me much admiration.
   Sir Char. Stand not amazed to see me thus
    attended:
Acton, I owe thee money, and being unable
To bring thee the full sum in ready coin,
Lo! for thy more assurance, here's a pawn,—
My sister, my dear sister, whose chaste honour
I prize above a million: here, nay, take her;
She's worth your money, man; do not forsake
    her.
   Sir Fran. I would he were in earnest!
   Susan. Impute it not to my immodesty;
My brother being rich in nothing else
But in his interest that he hath in me,
According to his poverty hath brought you
Me, all his store; whom howsoe'er you prize
As forfeit to your hand, he values highly,
And would not sell, but to acquit your debt,
For any emperor's ransom.
   Sir Fran. [*Aside.*] Stern heart, relent;
Thy former cruelty at length repent.
Was ever known, in any former age,
Such honourable wrested courtesy?
Lands, honours, life, and all the world forego,
Rather than stand engaged to such a foe.
   Sir Char. Acton, she is too poor to be thy bride,
And I too much opposed to be thy brother.
There, take her to thee: if thou hast the heart

To seize her as a rape, or lustful prey;
To blur our house that never yet was stained;
To murder her that never meant thee harm;
To kill me now, whom once thou savedst from
    death,
Do them at once; on her all these rely,
 And perish with her spotted chastity.
   Sir Fran. You overcome me in your love, Sir
    Charles;
I cannot be so cruel to a lady
I love so dearly.   Since you have not spared
To engage your reputation to the world,
Your sister's honour, which you prize so dear,
Nay, all the comforts which you hold on earth,
To grow out of my debt, being your foe,
Your honoured thoughts, lo! thus I recompense:
Your metamorphosed foe receives your gift
In satisfaction of all former wrongs.
This jewel I will wear here in my heart;
And, where before I thought her for her wants
Too base to be my bride, to end all strife,
I seal you my dear brother, her my wife.
   Susan. You still exceed us: I will yield to fate,
And learn to love, where I till now did hate.
   Sir Char. With that enchantment you have
    charmed my soul,
And made me rich even in those very words:.
I pay no debt, but am indebted more;
Rich in your love, I never can be poor.
   Sir Fran. All's mine is yours; we are alike in
    state,
Let's knit in love what was opposed in hate.
Come! for our nuptials we will straight provide,
Blest only in our brother and fair bride.   [*Exeunt.*

Enter CRANWELL, FRANKFORD, *and* NICHOLAS.

   Cran. Why do you search each room about
     your house,
Now that you have despatched your wife away?
   Frank. O sir, to see that nothing may be left
That ever was my wife's. I loved her dearly,
And when I do but think of her unkindness,
My thoughts are all in hell; to avoid which
     torment,
I would not have a bodkin or a cuff,
A bracelet, necklace, or rebato[18] wire;
Nor any thing that ever was called hers,
Left me, by which I might remember her.
Seek round about.
   Nic. 'Sblood, master! here's her lute flung in
     a corner.
   Frank. Her lute! O God! upon this instrument
Her fingers have run quick division,
Sweeter than that which now divides our hearts.
These frets have made me pleasant, that have
     now
Frets of my heart-strings made. O Master
     Cranwell,
Oft hath she made this melancholy wood,
Now mute and dumb for her disastrous chance,
Speak sweetly many a note, sound many a strain
To her own ravishing voice, which being well
     strung,
What pleasant strange airs have they jointly
     rung !
Post with it after her. Now nothing's left;
Of her and hers, I am at once bereft.
   Nic. I'll ride and overtake her; do my message,

[18] A rebato was a species of plaited ruff which turned
back and lay on the shoulders.

And come back again.

 Cran. Mean time, sir, if you please,
I'll to Sir Francis Acton, and inform him
Of what hath passèd betwixt you and his sister.

 Frank. Do as you please. How ill am I bested,
To be a widower ere my wife be dead!

Enter Mistress FRANKFORD, *with* JENKIN, CICELY,
 her Coachman, *and three* Carters.

 Anne. Bid my coach stay: why should I ride
  in state,
Being hurled so low down by the hand of fate?
A seat like to my fortunes let me have;
Earth for my chair, and for my bed a grave.

 Jenk. Comfort, good mistress; you have
watered your coach with tears already: you have
but two mile now to go to your manor. A man
cannot say by my old master Frankford as he
may say by me, that he wants manors, for he
hath three or four, of which this is one that we
are going to now.

 Cicely. Good mistress, be of good cheer;
sorrow, you see, hurts you, but helps you not:
we all mourn to see you so sad.

 Carter. Mistress, I spy one of my landlord's
  men
Come riding post: 'tis like he brings some news.

 Anne. Comes he from Master Frankford, he is
  welcome;
So are his news because they come from him.

Enter NICHOLAS.

 Nic. [*He hands her the lute.*] There.

 Anne. I know the lute; oft have I sung to thee:
We both are out of tune, both out of time.

Nic. Would that had been the worst instrument
that e'er you played on. My master commends
him to ye; there's all he can find that was ever
yours: he hath nothing left that ever you could
lay·claim to but his own heart, and he could
afford you that. All that I have to deliver you is
this: he prays you to forget him, and so he bids
you farewell.

Anne. I thank him: he is kind, and ever wàs.
All you that have true feeling of my grief,
That know my loss, and have relenting hearts,
Gird me about, and help me with your tears
To wash my spotted sins: mv lute shall groan;
It cannot weep, but shall lament my moan.

       Enter WENDOLL (*who remains unseen.*)

Wen. Pursued with horror of a guilty soul,
And with the sharp scourge of repentance lashed
I fly from my own shadow. O my stars!
What have my parents in their lives deserved,
That you should lay this penance on their son?
When I but think of Master Frankford's love,
And lay it to my treason, or compare
My murdering him for his relieving me,
It strikes a terror like a lightning's flash
To scorch my blood up. Thus I, like the owl,
Ashamed of day, live in these shadowy woods,
Afraid of every leaf or murmuring blast,
Yet longing to receive some perfect knowledge
How he hath dealt with her. O my sad fate!
Here, and so far from home, and thus attended!
O God! I have divorced the truest turtles
That ever lived together; and, being divided
In several places, make their several moan;
She in the fields laments, and he at home.
So poets write that Orpheus made the trees

And stones to dance to his melodious harp,
Meaning the rustic and the barbarous hinds,
That had no understanding part in them :
So she from these rude carters tears extracts,
Making their flinty hearts with grief to rise,
And draw down rivers from their rocky eyes.
    Anne. [*To* NICHOLAS.] If you return unto your
      master, say
(Though not from me; for I am all unworthy
To blast his name so with a strumpet's tongue)
That you have seen me weep, wish myself dead.
Nay, you may say too (for my vow is passed)
Last night you saw me eat and drink my last.
This to your master you may say and swear ;
For it is writ in Heaven, and decreed here.
    Nic. I'll say you wept : I'll swear you made me
      sad.
Why how now, eyes? what now? what's here to
      do?
I'm gone, or I shall straight turn baby too.
    Wen. I cannot weep, my heart is all on fire :
Curst be the fruits of my unchaste desire !
    Anne. Go, break this lute upon my coach's
      wheel,
As the last music that I e'er shall make ;
Not as my husband's gift, but my farewell
To all earth's joy ; and so your master tell.
    Nic. If I can for crying.
    Wen. Grief, have done,
Or like a madman I shall frantic run.
    Anne. You have beheld the wofullest wretch on
      earth ;
A woman made of tears : would you had words
To express but what you see ! My inward grief
No tongue can utter ; yet unto your power
You may describe my sorrow, and disclose
To thy sad master my abundant woes.

Nic. I'll do your commendations.

Anne. Oh no:
I dare not so presume; nor to my children:
I am disclaimed in both; alas, I am.
Oh, never teach them, when they come to speak,
To name the name of Mother: chide their tongue,
If they by chance light on that hated word;
Tell them 'tis naught; for, when that word they
     name,
(Poor pretty souls) they harp on their own shame.

     Wen. To recompense her wrongs, what canst
     thou do?
Thou hast made her husbandless and childless too.

     Anne. I have no more to say. Speak not for
     me;
Yet you may tell your master what you see.

     Nic. I'll do't.   [*Exit.*

     Wen. I'll speak to her, and comfort her in
     grief.
Oh! but her wound cannot be cured with words.
No matter though, I'll do my best good-will
To work a cure on her whom I did kill.

     Anne. So, now unto my coach, then to my
     home,
So to my death-bed; for from this sad hour
I never will nor eat, nor drink, nor taste
Of any cates that may preserve my life:
I never will nor smile, nor sleep, nor rest;
But when my tears have washed my black soul
     white,
Sweet Saviour, to Thy hands I yield my sprite.

     Wen. O Mistress Frankford—

     Anne. Oh, for God's sake fly!
The devil doth come to tempt me ere I die.
My coach! this fiend, that with an angel's face
Conjured mine honour, till he sought my wrack,
In my repentant eyes seems ugly black.

[Exeunt all, except Wendoll *and* Jenkin;
the Carters *whistling.*

Jenk. What, my young master that fled in his shirt! How come you by your clothes again? You have made our house in a sweet pickle, ha' ye not, think you? What, shall I serve you still, or cleave to the old house?

Wen. Hence, slave! away with thy unseasoned mirth!
Unless thou canst shed tears, and sigh, and howl,
Curse thy sad fortunes, and exclaim on fate,
Thou art not for my turn.

Jenk. Marry, an you will not, another will: farewell, and be hanged! Would you had never come to have kept this coil within our doors; we shall ha' you run away like a sprite again.

Wen. She's gone to death; I live to want and woe;
Her life, her sins, and all upon my head.
And I must now go wander, like a Cain,
In foreign countries and remoted climes,
Where the report of my ingratitude
Cannot be heard. I'll over first to France,
And so to Germany and Italy;
Where when I have recovered, and by travel
Gotten those perfect tongues, and that these rumours
May in their height abate, I will return:
And I divine (however now dejected)
My worth and parts being by some great man praised,
At my return I may in court be raised.   *[Exit.*

Enter Sir Francis, Sir Charles, Cranwell,
Malby *and* Susan.

Sir Fran. Brother, and now my wife, I think these troubles

Fall on my head by justice of the heavens,
For being so strict to you in your extremities :
But we are now atoned.   I would my sister
Could with like happiness o'ercome her griefs,
As we have ours.
   Susan. You tell us, Master Cranwell, wondrous
     things,
Touching the patience of that gentleman,
With what strange virtue he demeans his grief.
   Cran. I told you what I was a witness of ;
It was my fortune to lodge there that night.
   Sir Fran. O that same villain Wendoll! 'twas
     his tongue
That did corrupt her ; she was of herself
Chaste and devoted well.   Is this the house?
   Cran. Yes, sir, I take it here your sister lies.
   Sir Fran. My brother Frankford showed too
     mild a spirit
In the revenge of such a loathèd crime ;
Less than he did, no man of spirit could do :
I am so far from blaming his revenge,
That I commend it.   Had it been my case,
Their souls at once had from their breasts been
     freed :
Death to such deeds of shame is the due meed.

Enter JENKIN *and* CICELY.

   Jenk. O my mistress, my mistress, my poor
mistress !
   Cicely. Alas that ever I was born ! what shall
I do for my poor mistress?
   Sir Char. Why, what of her?
   Jenk. O Lord, sir, she no sooner heard that her
brother and his friends were come to see how she
did, but she, for very shame of her guilty con-

science, fell into such a swoon, that we had much
ado to get life into her.

    Susan. Alas, that she should bear so hard a
      fate!
Pity it is repentance comes too late.
    Sir Fran. Is she so weak in body?
    Jenk. O sir, I can assure you there's no hope
of life in her, for she will take no sustenance:
she hath plainly starved herself, and now she is
as lean as a lath. She ever looks for the good
hour. Many gentlemen and gentlewomen of the
country are come to comfort her.   *[Exeunt.*

    Enter Mistress FRANKFORD *in her Bed.*

    Mal. How fare you, Mistress Frankford?
    Anne. Sick, sick, oh, sick. Give me some air
      I pray you.
Tell me, oh, tell me where is Master Frankford?
Will not he deign to see me ere I die?
    Mal. Yes, Mistress Frankford: divers gentle-
      men,
Your loving neighbours, with that just request
Have moved, and told him of your weak estate:
Who, though with much ado to get belief,
Examining of the general circumstance,
Seeing your sorrow and your penitence,
And hearing therewithal the great desire
You have to see him ere you left the world,
He gave to us his faith to follow us,
And sure he will be here immediately.
    Anne. You have half revived me with those
      pleasing news:
Raise me a little higher in my bed.
Blush I not, brother Acton? Blush I not, Sir
      Charles?
Can you not read my fault writ in my cheek?

Is not my crime there? tell me, gentlemen.

  Sir Char. Alas! good mistress, sickness hath
    not left you

Blood in your face enough to make you blush.

  Anne. Then sickness, like a friend, my fault
    would hide.

Is my husband come? My soul but tarries

His arrive, then I am fit for Heaven.

  Sir Fran. I came to chide you; but my words of
    hate

Are turned to pity and compassionate grief.

I came to rate you; but my brawls, you see,

Melt into tears, and I must weep by thee.

Here's Master Frankford now.

Enter FRANKFORD.

  Frank. Good-morrow, brother; morrow, gen-
    tlemen:

God, that hath laid this cross upon our heads,

Might (had He pleased) have made our cause of
    meeting

On a more fair and more contented ground;

But He that made us, made us to this woe.

  Anne. And is he come? Methinks that voice
    I know.

  Frank. How do you, woman?

  Anne. Well, Master Frankford, well; but shall
    be better,

I hope, within this hour. Will you vouchsafe

(Out of your grace and your humanity)

To take a spotted strumpet by the hand?

  Frank. This hand once held my heart in faster
    bonds

Than now 'tis gripped by me. God pardon them

That made us first break hold!

  Anne. Amen, amen.

Out of my zeal to Heaven, whither I'm now
    bound,
I was so impudent to wish you here;
And once more beg your pardon. Oh, good man,
And father to my children, pardon me,
Pardon, oh, pardon me! My fault so heinous is,
That if you in this world forgive it not,
Heaven will not clear it in the world to come.
Faintness hath so usurped upon my knees
That kneel I cannot, but on my heart's knees
My prostrate soul lies thrown down at your feet
To beg your gracious pardon. Pardon, oh, par-
    don me!
    Frank. As freely, from the low depth of my
    soul,
As my Redeemer hath forgiven His death,
I pardon thee. I will shed tears for thee, pray
    with thee;
And, in mere pity of thy weak estate,
I'll wish to die with thee.
    All. So do we all.
    Nic. So will not I;
I'll sigh and sob, but, by my faith, not die.
    Sir Fran. O master Frankford, all the near
    alliance
I lose by her shall be supplied in thee:
You are my brother by the nearest way;
Her kindred hath fallen off, but yours doth stay.
    Frank. Even as I hope for pardon at that day
When the great Judge of Heaven in scarlet sits,
So be thou pardoned. Though thy rash offence
Divorced our bodies, thy repentant tears
Unite our souls.
    Sir Char. Then comfort, Mistress Frankford;
You see your husband hath forgiven your fall;
Then rouse your spirits, and cheer your fainting
    soul.

Susan. How is it with you?

Sir Fran. How do ye feel yourself?

Anne. Not of this world.

Frank. I see you are not, and I weep to see it.
My wife, the mother to my pretty babes!
Both those lost names I do restore thee back,
And with this kiss I wed thee once again :
Though thou art wounded in thy honoured name,
And with that grief upon thy death-bed liest,
Honest in heart, upon my soul, thou diest.

Anne. Pardoned on earth, soul, thou in Heaven
  art free.
Once more thy wife, dies thus embracing thee.

Frank. New married, and new widowed. Oh!
  she's dead,
And a cold grave must be her nuptial bed.

Sir Char. Sir, be of good comfort; and your
  heavy sorrow
Part equally amongst us : storms divided
Abate their force, and with less rage are guided.

Cran. Do, Master Frankford : he that hath
  least part
Will find enough to drown one troubled heart.

Sir Fran. Peace with thee, Nan. Brothers,
  and gentlemen,
(All we that can plead interest in her grief)
Bestow upon her body funeral tears.
Brother, had you with threats and usage bad
 Punished her sin, the grief of her offence
Had not with such true sorrow touched her heart.

Frank. I see it had not : therefore on her grave
Will I bestow this funeral epitaph,
Which on her marble tomb shall be engraved.
In golden letters shall these words be filled,
Here lies she whom her husband's kindness killed.

THE EPILOGUE

An honest Crew, disposèd to be merry,
   Come to a Tavern by, and called for wine:
The Drawer brought it, smiling like a Cherry,
   And told them it was pleasant, neat, and fine.
"Taste it," quoth one. He did so. "Fie!"
   quoth he;
"This wine was good; now't runs too near the
   Lee."

Another sipped, to give the wine his due,
   And said unto the rest it drunk too flat;
The third said, it was old; the fourth, too new;
   Nay, quoth the fifth, the sharpness likes me not.
Thus, Gentlemen, you see how, in one hour,
The wine was new, old, flat, sharp, sweet, and
   sour.

Unto this wine we do allude our play;
   Which some will judge too trivial, some too
   grave:
You as our Guests we entertain this day,
   And bid you welcome to the best we have:
Excuse us, then; Good wine may be disgraced,
When every several mouth hath sundry taste.

PRINTED BY
F. J. MANSFIELD,
ERITH, S.E.

Novels at 6s.

Crown 8vo. Bound in uniform Red Cloth with Gold Panel Back.

The Wisdom of the Serpent
By Constantine Ralli.

The Return of Joe, and other New Zealand Stories
By W. H. Koebel.

Love a la Mode
By Kineton Parkes.

Passing down the Avenues
By L. Rutherfoord Skey.

A Stranger within the Gates
By F. J. Cox.

Love in London
By A. St. John Adcock.

Where Two Worlds Met
By Sydney Phelps and Bridey M. O'Reilly.

The Mantle of the Emperor
By Ladbroke Black and Robert Lynd. With Twelve Illustrations by Paul Henry.

London : FRANCIS GRIFFITHS, 34, Maiden Lane, Strand, W.C

SONGS OF THE CAR;

With "DE OMNIBUS" RHYMES.

By F. J. Cox.   Illustrated by Howard Somerville.

Crown 8vo.   Cloth.   3/6 net.

OPINIONS OF THE PRESS.

"DAILY CHRONICLE."—" Mr. F. J. Cox's clever verses. Many of these we have already met in the columns of 'Mr. Punch'; and are glad to meet again. Mr. Cox has wit and humour; and the means of expressing both."

"SPECTATOR."—" Mr. Cox is a skilful writer of humorous verse. . . . Not the least of his many gifts is the ingenuity of his rhymes."

"MORNING LEADER."—" His verses not infrequently contain the soul of wit. Whether as parodist (the motor parodies are particularly happy), or as original composer of frivolity, he is a most diverting companion. His technique is versatile and finished, his humour agile, pointed, and never bitter. These scattered verses were well worth collecting."

"SCOTSMAN."—" The verses are funny, so there is no need to to argue about them. There are, besides, more pieces in the book than those about the auto—pieces about St. Valentine, about ladies' names, about the pretensions of the Celtic renascent poets, and, in a word, about everything in general and nothing in particular, all of which reveal an agreeable humour and a curious felicity in spinning dainty arabesques of society verse. The good comic effect of the book is well helped out by Mr. Somerville's illustrations, graphical compositions of a lucidity and point akin to those of the verses."

London : FRANCIS GRIFFITHS, 34, Maiden Lane, Strand, W.C.

CPSIA information can be obtained
at www.ICGtesting.com
Printed in the USA
LVOW10s1939190917
549279LV00011B/984/P